Basic Java Programming

A Laboratory Approach

Joe Kent & Lewis Barnett

University of Richmond

Franklin, Beedle & Associates
8536 SW St. Helens Drive, Suite D
Wilsonville, OR 97070
(503) 682-7668
www.fbeedle.com

President and Publisher   Jim Leisy (jimleisy@fbeedle.com)
Developmental Editor   Sue Page
Manuscript Editor   Stephanie Welch
Production   Stephanie Welch
                           Tom Sumner

Cover Design   Ian Shadburne
Marketing   Chris Collier
Order Processing   Lois Allison
                           Krista Hall

Printed in the U.S.A.

Library of Congress Cataloging-in-Publication Data

Kent, Joe.
    Basic Java programming : a laboratory approach / Joe Kent & Lewis Barnett.
        p. cm.
    ISBN 1-887902-67-8
        1. Java (Computer program language) 2. Computer science--Laboratory manuals. I.
    Barnett, Lewis. II. Title.

    QA76.73.J38 K46 2001
    005.13'3--dc21

                                                          2001025399

Table of Contents

iii

Laboratory 6—Zip Codes and Postal Bar Codes 68

Focusing on the creation of small utility functions and procedures, this laboratory examines the coding and decoding of postal bar codes. You will learn how to write methods that can be used multiple times to solve problems. A large program to perform the coding and decoding provides a graphics display but depends on these small methods to work properly. You will complete these methods in the laboratory session.

Laboratory 7—A Methods Toolbox 75

Continuing the focus on methods and procedures, you will develop a number of static methods within a Toolbox class. These methods then can be reused later as required. This lab will prompt you to think about writing program components that will be reused.

Laboratory 8—Collections. 87

In all programming languages, arrays are an essential data organization. In this laboratory arrays are introduced and explored with simple examples. The post-laboratory provides a brief look at the Vector class. Some simple methods involving arrays will be written and added to your Toolbox class.

Laboratory 9—Drawing with Java. 100

This laboratory uses methods of the Graphics object associated with a Canvas to create images. Using the principles of object-oriented programming, you will construct classes for rectangles, triangles, circles, and other special shapes. The post-laboratory extends this work to the creation of images for playing-card symbols—a heart, a spade, a diamond, and a club. The created classes all implement a simple interface illustrating the principle of common behavior among a collection of classes.

Laboratory 10—Recursive Methods 119

Simple principles of recursive functions and procedures are explored with examples. The recursive creation of graphics images using simple drawing is illustrated, together with the classic recursive method to find the greatest common divisor of two integers. A recursive version of the selection sort is tested. The laboratory will ask you to study and run some programs, as well as to write new programs using the recursive model presented in the pre-laboratory examples.

Laboratory 11—Linear Algorithms 128

Linear search, binary search, and sorting are the key topics of this laboratory. The two searches are implemented and tested, as is an iterative version of selection sort. The concept of algorithm efficiency is introduced in the pre-laboratory reading, where linear search and binary search are compared. Methods that implement these algorithms will be added to your Toolbox class.

Laboratory 12—Sorting Out Sorts 136

The merge sort algorithm is introduced and compared with selection sort. In the laboratory you will code a merge sort and then time the two sort algorithms on large data sets to determine if the empirical results support the claims of efficiency.

Laboratory 13—I/O and Exceptions 144

We have used LabPkg prior to this laboratory to avoid dealing with the problems of input from the keyboard. The focus of this laboratory is processing data from files and from the console. Both require the introduction of exception handling, exceptions, and the try-catch mechanism. Most of the attention is centered on file processing in Java.

Preface

Learning to Program

Programming requires careful analysis of a problem followed by the design of a solution. Only then is the design implemented, using an appropriate programming language. Java is a relatively new programming language; it is object-oriented and is a popular choice for Web applications. It will be the implementation language for these laboratories.

Learning to program requires

- learning the syntax and semantics of a programming language,
- paying attention to details, and
- developing design solutions for given problems.

For beginners the first two components seem to dominate, while the problems to be solved often seem contrived and unrealistic. This is natural. If you were taking a beginning Spanish class, you would have to learn basic vocabulary and use it with correct grammar in spoken and written situations. Initially your conversations would be simple: "Good morning. How are you?" "Can you tell me where to find the train station?" "Do you have a room with a shower available?" "How much is the bill?" The more sophisticated expression of ideas would have to wait until the basics were mastered and vocabulary was expanded.

This text will provide a firm foundation for advanced topics in computer science—moving from solving basic problems with Java to using object-oriented design to implement a sophisticated computer game.

These materials are designed to be a hands-on learning experience. For that reason, each "chapter" is called a "laboratory." Each lab will include some preliminary discussion of the topics covered, allowing the book to be used as both textbook and laboratory manual for those who want to develop programming skills in Java outside of a formal educational environment.

Coverage

This book incorporates materials intended for use in an introductory programming course. The intended audience is first- or second-year college students with no prior experience in programming. In national curricular reports, the topics included in this text comprise the generic CS1 course, the first course for prospective computer science majors.

The text also provides a rapid hands-on introduction to Java. Computer science is more than just programming, so we introduce some important algorithms and problem-solving approaches and preview advanced topics such as event-driven programming. Our goal is to build a firm foundation for continued work in computer science, while providing glimpses of more advanced topics.

Assumptions

No previous programming experience is assumed. We do assume basic computer literacy—familiarity with basic tools and commands to create folders, copy files, and use a Web browser. In formal educational settings, your instructor may provide a preliminary guided experience to introduce you to the local computer laboratory environment. Of course, the process of creating, compiling, and running programming will be explained in the first lab.

We would like these labs to be independent of any computer environment, but that is not totally possible. We assume the environment to be Microsoft's Windows 95/98/NT/2000.

IDEs

It is possible to create Java programs using a simple editor like Notepad and the tools of the free Java Development Kit (now called the SDK) from Sun Microsystems, but that approach is relatively primitive. A number of integrated development environments, or IDEs, are available. These are applications that use a graphical user interface to provide windows, menus, buttons, and so on to aid in program development and testing. We prefer Kawa by Allaire (`http://www.allaire.com/products/kawa/index.cfm`) because it allows for easy creation of very simple programs and can be used with any version of Java. However, we have made every attempt to make this manual IDE-independent. An appendix covers the basics of several common IDEs that support Java™ 2. Only the first laboratory uses the Kawa IDE's steps for compiling and running a program. These steps are easily replaced by those of other IDEs, using the appendix materials.

LabPkg

We want these labs to be as independent as possible of any particular book. For that reason we have developed a Java package, `LabPkg`, that we use for our applications. The package allows your programs to interact with the user via graphical components. The critical class is ViewFrame, which is instantiated as a window with three components:

- a toolbar with a provided "Exit" button that kills the current application
- a scrolled text area for displaying program output
- a "canvas" for displaying images or drawing figures

The canvas component is optional and is not used in most simple applications. The user may add additional buttons to the toolbar for initiating actions. Interactive input is obtained by pop-up dialog windows generated by calls to simple methods.

If you looked at another text, it would have a different package, as every author has a favorite way to do input in Java. Why? Java supports input from the keyboard on a line-by-line basis, but forces the user to process the string of characters to extract the desired numeric values and handle errors. For beginners the details of this task distract from the primary goal of understanding principles of programming that apply generally. Special packages hide the mess. Unfortunately, there is no standard package at this time.

Our package is based on the paradigm of a program as having three components: the model, the view, and the controller. (This is the MVC paradigm developed by Smalltalk programmers more than 20 years ago.) The *model* is simply the data that represents the current state of the program. The *view* is what the user sees of the data. The *controller* is the part that provides interaction of the user with the program. Often the view and controller components are joined in programs that use a graphical user interface. For most of our programs a ViewFrame object provides the view and controller components.

Appendix A provides information about the package and its use, with simple examples.

Getting Files

A diskette accompanies the text and contains all the files required for the laboratories, plus example programs discussed in the pre-lab readings. The file `index.html` provides a guide to the files and documentation and should be opened in a browser.

Using a browser, the files can be "downloaded" by the student from the diskette to a local hard drive or a network drive. It is also possible to use Windows Explorer to copy the files from the diskette. The files are in subfolders of the folder `labfiles`.

The diskette contains information concerning setting up a personal computer to do the hands-on part of the text.

The Authors

We are computer science faculty at the University of Richmond, with more than 38 combined years of teaching experience. We developed early Java versions of these laboratories as special experiences for our students more than five years ago. In the fall of 1999 they were expanded and used in a formal laboratory setting. Experience and feedback from other faculty allowed us to refine those initial materials.

Thanks

We would like to thank faculty colleagues who provided feedback: Anita Hubbard, Gary Greenfield, and Arthur Charlesworth. Special thanks go to Jim Leisy, our editor, who had faith in us. Of course, we cannot forget the hundreds of students at UR who provided candid responses to their experiences with the materials.

For supporting us while we worked on the manuscript, we give special thanks to our wives, Mary Kent and Rebekah Barnett.

1

Computational Java

This laboratory is designed to get you quickly writing or modifying Java programs using an *integrated development environment,* or *IDE.* We will introduce the collection of useful classes that are provided with the labs and demonstrate their use in simple programs.

This lab is entitled "Computational Java" because it illustrates arithmetic operations in Java. Later laboratories will focus more on the object-oriented features of Java. These initial examples will be simple. Our goal is the successful writing of programs and mastery of the process using an IDE.

Start by reading the pre-lab discussion of a minimal Java program, declarations, and expressions.

Key Diskette File

You may want to insert the diskette that comes with the text into your computer as you read the material. It contains documentation as well as access to all the files used in the laboratories. The key file is `A:\index.html` (assuming your diskette drive is the `A:` drive), which can be opened in your Web browser.

Pre-Laboratory Reading

Programs and Programming

A computer program is traditionally said to be a sequence of instructions for performing a task, with the instructions specified in a special language that can be understood by the computer. The programmer must not only specify the desired behavior of the computer, but also explicitly tell the computer how to do the desired task.

Types of Programs

There are, roughly, two types of programs:
- sequential or task-oriented
- event-driven or interactive

The first type starts, performs its task, and terminates. The second type starts, waits for events to occur, responds to events, and waits for more events. This second type is typical of most modern applications. Just think of a simple computer solitaire game. The user clicks on a card or drags a card from one pile to another. The mouse press is an event, as is the mouse release. Even the movement of the mouse generates events that report its location. If you walk away from the game to get lunch, the program waits patiently for you to come back and generate another event. The program's response to these events depends on the particular event, but generally the state of the game is changed (perhaps a card is reassigned to a new pile) and the board is "repainted" on the screen with the changes.

Within event-driven programs are sections of instructions that are task-oriented, so writing the first type of program is still valuable. In fact, nearly all textbooks for beginners focus on the first model: start—do something—stop. We try to keep the second model close at hand with examples. But the second model requires more sophistication to get correct, so a careful examination of event-driven programming will wait until later laboratories.

The Creation Process

The creation of a computer program involves a number of steps:
1. Specify the problem in an unambiguous manner.
2. Design a solution.
3. Implement the solution as a program by creating one or more files written in a programming language like Java.
4. Translate each of the program files into a form understandable by a machine (this is called "compilation"), correcting any errors of grammar that are detected.
5. Test the compiled program by running it with typical and atypical inputs to see if the design solution is logically sound. If errors are found, return to the second step, fix the solution, and redo the implementation.
6. Release the program for public use.
7. Add new features upon request. This requires a restarting of the entire process and is called the "maintenance" phase.

For very small programs, the second and third steps may be combined, but for programs of any size and complexity, the second step is critical and requires a significant amount of time. If the design is sound, implementation will be easy and testing will be quick.

To write your first program, it is not hard to go through the first two steps, but what do you do at step 3? How do you actually write your solution in Java, compile it, and run it? The answer is to use one of the many integrated development environments (IDEs) available. Examples are JBuilder, CodeWarrior, Visual J++, VisualCafé, and Kawa. Each has an editor to allow you to type in the program instructions. Each has menu selections that compile the current file. Each allows you to organize your program files into a project—useful if the program is large and has many files. Each has menu selections that execute the program. Each has a "debugger," a way to run a program in a controlled manner that allows the programmer to see all changes to data as they occur.

Appendix B contains basic information for selected IDEs that support Java™ 2 program development. For each IDE we indicate the commands and steps for

- creating and editing a Java program file
- creating a project if that is required
- compiling a file and an entire project
- running a compiled program

In this initial laboratory we will use the Kawa IDE. If you are using another IDE you will want to keep the appropriate page from Appendix B handy.

Now let's look at the Java language basics.

Basic Java Revealed

The first thing you should understand is the form of a *minimal* Java program like the one shown below.

```
// Minimal.java (this is a comment containing the file name)
//          YOUR NAME GOES HERE
//  A description comes next
public class  Minimal
{
    public static void main(String[] args)
    {
        // statements go here
    }
}
```

Any line or part of a line that begins with // is considered a *comment* and is ignored by the computer. Comments are for programmers' notes. In our example, the first three lines are comments. Usually, it is useful to indicate the name of the file so references are easier when you are dealing with hard copies (printed copies). It is also important to include your name! Of course, you can have additional comment lines if you want to keep more notes.

Every Java file has a single "public class," **which must have the same name as the file** (without the .java).

The main Method

A Java program can be composed of *many* files, but only one contains the special method:[1]

```
public static void main(String[] args)
{
```

---

1. A method is a function, i.e., a named collection of statements. It has parentheses immediately after the name that can be used to provide data used by the statements. Methods can simply do work or produce a value. The main method simply does work. The keyword void tells us that it does not produce a value.

```
     . . . .
}
```

The class that contains this method is referred to as the "main" class. This method is where program execution begins! The meanings of terms like "public," "static," "void," and "String[] args" are initially cryptic, but will become clear within a few weeks. For now, think of this as a "boiler plate" that you will use in all of the programs you write.

Of course, some words are naturally suggestive of their meaning. For example, "public" means that we can request the execution of the method from outside the enclosing class. This process is referred to as "calling" the method. "void" means that the method does some work but does not return a value like an integer or a character.

In Java, "String" refers to a block of characters like a word or sentence. "String[]" refers to a collection of String blocks and "args" is the name that is used to refer to this collection. In most examples, we don't use "args" within our programs, but Java requires that it be listed nonetheless.

Java Output

The most basic Java operation that produces *output* is

```
System.out.println("xxxxxxxx");
```

where xxxxxxxx can be replaced by any collection of characters (just avoid quotation marks for now). System.out is a Java object that accesses a special text output window (or the console screen if you are working in a command line setting). The method println() expects a String inside its parentheses. Any quoted block of characters is a *literal* String.

Please note that the *fully qualified name* of the method above is System.out.println. The parentheses indicate a method in such a context. **Any simple statement *must* be terminated with a semicolon.**

Variables and Declarations

Programs often compute values, save values for later use, and display values on the screen. Values can be of many types, and they are often stored in the computer's memory. *Variables* are symbolic names for references to values. All variables must be *declared* as to the type of value they refer to.

Java has two categories of values:
- primitive types
- references to objects

The most common primitive types are

```
int  - for an integer or whole number value
double- for a number with a decimal point like 2.34
char - for a single character value
```

Typical variable declarations might look like

```
int a;
int x = 5,  y = 0;
double myPi = 3.14;
```

In the first case we declare an integer variable a without an explicit initial value. In the second case we declare two variables, x and y, to hold integer values *and* give them starting values of 5 and 0 respectively. In the third case we declare a variable called myPi and give it the starting value of 3.14. **Notice that all declarations end in a semicolon.**

Rule: Prior to its first use, a variable must be declared. The basic format is

```
type   variable_name ;
```

An alternative format combines the declaration with the specification of an initial value.

```
type  variable_name = initial_value ;
```

The alternative format is a convenience only. Java does require that a variable be given an initial value prior to use of that variable in an expression.

After a variable's declaration, its type is known. It need not be repeated. For example,

```
int  x;
x = 5;      // not int x = 5; as we have already declared x
while (x > 0)    // not while (int x > 0)
{
   ....
}
```

Don't worry about the meaning of the while statement. Simply note that x is used and compared with 0, but the int type is not repeated.

Spacing is not critical in Java. The only rule is that keywords and variable names cannot have spaces, tabs, or carriage returns in them. The following is fine, but not as concise as int x = 123;:

```
int
   x
              =
123            ;
```

Assignments and Expressions

Once declared, a variable can be used to change itself and other values via expressions involving arithmetic.

```
y = 17 + 5 * x;
```

This statement replaces the value of y with 5 times the current value of x plus 17. The multiplication is done before the addition. Any prior value of y is erased by the new value.

This is an example of an *assignment statement,* as y is "assigned" a new value. **A single equal sign (=) is used to indicate assignment.** The right-hand side of the statement is an expression.

The expression x + 6 has the value of x plus 6 more, as you might expect. It does not change the value of x in any way. However, the assignment statement

```
x = x + 6;
```

does change the value of x, because x is assigned the result of its old value plus 6.

Rule: In an assignment statement, the right-hand side of the expression is evaluated first, and then the result is assigned to the variable on the left-hand side.

Evaluating Expressions

Arithmetic expressions involve variables, constants, and functions that produce numeric values, in addition to the usual special symbols for operations (+, -, *, /, and %). Parentheses are used to group expression components to determine the order of evaluation.

The definitions of addition (+), subtraction (-), multiplication (*), and unary minus (-) are as they are in arithmetic, but division (/) and the remainder operation (%) need special comment.

The result of division depends on the types of the operands.

- If both are integers (int), then the result must be an integer formed by ignoring any remainder. Hence, 15 / 4 is 3.

- If either operand is a type with a decimal point, then the result will be precise and with a decimal point. Therefore, `15 / 4.0` is `3.75`.

The remainder operator requires that both operands be integers. `15 % 7` is 1, as 15 equals `2 * 7 + 1`. Also, `38 % 2` is 0, as 38 equals `19 * 2 + 0`. (For now we will restrict ourselves to positive values. `-15 % 7` is `-1`, which seems to violate our grade-school concept of remainder as a non-negative value.)

Rules for Evaluation Order

In an expression involving several operators, *precedence* is the term for which operator is used first. If one operator has higher precedence than another, the one with the higher precedence is used first. In determining `5 - 3 * 2`, `3 * 2` is evaluated first, then `5 - 6`, because `*` has higher precedence than `-`. Parentheses in an expression can change the order of the evaluation of terms within the expression. The basic rules are the following:

- Evaluate expressions inside parentheses first. For nested parentheses, work from the innermost parenthesized expression to the outermost.
- `*`, `/`, and `%` have equal precedence.
- `+` and `-` have equal precedence, but their precedence is lower than `*`, `/`, and `%`.
- For expressions with more than one operator of the same precedence, in the absence of parentheses, the operations are evaluated from left to right.

Practice Exercise

Assume that `x` and `y` are `int` variables with values of 5 and 21, respectively. Assume that `z` is a `double` variable with the value 2.0. For each expression below, give the value that the computer would calculate:

```
x + y * 2
(x + y) * 2
x + y / 4
x + y / x - y
(x + y) / x - y
y - x - x * 2
y - (x - x * 2)
y / x
y / z
y % x
```

The Math Class

Java provides a number of special methods grouped into the Math class. These include most of the trigonometric functions, plus methods for the absolute value, the maximum of two values, the minimum of two values, the square root, raising a number to a power, and more.

If you are not familiar with the methods of the Math class, refer to the following Web page:[2]

```
http://www.javasoft.com/j2se/1.3/docs/api/index.html
```

(You may want to bookmark this in your browser so you can quickly return here.) Scroll down and click on the `java.lang` link (not java.math). When that page comes up, scroll down to `Math` and click on it. Now scroll down to the "Method Summary" section and examine the list. Notice that `abs()` appears multiple times, because the absolute value of an int is considered to be different

---

2. If the diskette that accompanies this text is inserted into the computer, you can double-click on the file `A:\index.html` in Windows Explorer to start your browser. Follow the links to the documentation that is available online for Java classes.

from the absolute value of a double value, i.e., these are different functions/ methods in Java. If you click on the method name, you get more information.

Using the values for x, y, and z from the previous exercise, what are the values of the following methods?

```
Math.abs(x - y)
Math.max(x, y)
Math.sqrt(16.0)
Math.pow(z, 3.0)  // raises z to the third power
Math.pow(z, z) / x
Math.sqrt(231.56005) * Math.sqrt(231.56005)
```

Roundoff Issues

The last expression above seems to have an obvious answer, but the computer may not give what you expect due to roundoff. A computer can only store a maximum number of digits when doing computation. Hence, `1.0 / 3.0` will be `0.33333333`, with the number of digits depending on the computer. Java guarantees the same precision on all computers, but even that doesn't solve the problem because `3.0 * 0.3333333` will never exactly equal `1.0`.

Warning: Be very careful when doing comparisons involving numbers with decimal points, because you may not get precise equality due to roundoff.

Boolean Data and Expressions

Java has a basic type known as `boolean`. The only possible boolean values are the special values `true` and `false`. You can declare boolean variables, as in

```
boolean found = false; // gives initial value of false
```

You can't do arithmetic with such variables, but you can do assignments, as in

```
found = true;
```

You also cannot read boolean data from the keyboard. Typing "true" (without quotation marks) at the keyboard input will be interpreted as typing a String instead of a boolean value.

Boolean expressions are more commonly used than boolean variables. A *boolean expression* is one that is true or false. There are a number of relational operators that are used in boolean expressions:

```
>   <   >=   <=   ==   !=   &&   ||   !
```

The first six listed are used with arithmetic expressions to compare values, as in

```
x > 0    // x has value greater than 0
y + z < x + 2 // y + z is less than x + 2
x >= 0   // x is greater than or equal to 0
y <= x   // y is less than or equal to x
y == x + 1  // y equals x + 1
x != 3     // x is not equal to 3
```

Each of these expressions is true or false depending on the values of x, y, and z.

Notice how we test for equality—with two equal signs. This is necessary, as we use a single equal sign for assignment. The remaining boolean operators `&&`, `||`, and `!` mean "and," "or," and "not," respectively.

Practice

Determine the value of the following expressions. If an expression is *not* boolean, say so. We assume that X is an integer variable with the value 45 and Y is an integer variable with the value -6.

```
X == Y
X < Y - 50      (Note: Y - 50 is computed first.)
X * Y <= 0
X != Y
X + Y
X > Y
X > -10
X = -10
```

Record your results. Be prepared to bring them to the lab session.

&&, | | , and !

Boolean expressions can be combined by using the operators && (meaning "and"), | | (meaning "or"), and ! (meaning "not"). The && has higher precedence than the | |. The ! operation has the highest precedence (without parentheses).

- The "and" of two boolean expressions is only true if *both* expressions are true.
- The "or" of two boolean expressions is true provided *either* one is true *or* both are true.
- "Not" simply changes the truth value to its opposite.

More Practice

Using the same values of X and Y as above, indicate the boolean value of these expressions:

```
X < 0 && Y > X                (Note: same as (X < 0) && (Y > X))
X == 5 || Y != X             (Same as (X == 5) || (Y != X))
!(X < 0)
!(X < 0 && Y < 0)
```

Packages and Java

Java comes with a large collection of prewritten program components. These components are special Java classes and allow the programmer to write sophisticated programs quickly without reinventing the wheel.

We have seen the special class Math. It is part of a collection of basic classes called java.lang. Also in this collection is the class String, which allows us to easily work with blocks of characters. **Java's collections of classes are called** *packages*.

The packages java.awt and javax.swing contain classes that support graphics programming in Java. For example, the classes Frame in java.awt and JFrame in javax.swing are both visualized as windows with the ability to support a menu bar and contain other graphical components. The full names of these classes are java.awt.Frame and javax.swing.JFrame. To avoid mentioning the full name, Java allows the programmer to write

```
import java.awt.*;
import javax.swing.*;
```

at the beginning of a program to indicate the possible use of a class from one of these packages. Then the programmer only has to refer to Frame or JFrame and not the full name.

It is not necessary to specify

```
import java.lang.*;
```

as Java programs automatically know about this fundamental package.

Our Special Package: LabPkg

Java encourages the programmer to create his or her own classes and to share them as packages. This improves productivity. One area where special packages have been used to avoid messy details is the area of Java input. Output is less problematic.

We are providing a package called *LabPkg*[3] that supports a graphical interface for your program. Its use saves the programmer from dealing with more

---

3.   For more details, see Appendix A.

complicated input and output mechanisms. The key class is called `ViewFrame`. A simple use is shown below:

```
import LabPkg.*;

public class Square
{
    public static void main(String[] args)
    {
        ViewFrame vf = new ViewFrame();
        vf.setVisible(true);
        int n;
        n = vf.readInt("Enter a whole number");
        int square;
        square = n * n;
        vf.println("The square is " + square);
    }
}
```

The `import` statement gives access to all the classes in the LabPkg package. If the programmer wanted to add a Button or use a Canvas, it would be necessary to add these import statements:

```
import java.awt.*;
import java.awt.event.*;
import javax.swing.*;
```

The program does only five things:
- creates a ViewFrame object and assigns it to the variable `vf`
- tells the ViewFrame object to make itself visible on the screen
- uses a ViewFrame method to pop up a dialog box and obtain an integer from the user (done by `vf.readInt("...")`)
- performs the calculation of the square of the integer
- displays a message in the output area of the ViewFrame object

The `new ViewFrame()` expression *creates* a ViewFrame object. After that we can use this object by calling its methods, as in `vf.println(...)`.

ViewFrame is the centerpiece of the package. It allows the programmer to have a visual component that can be used to obtain input and display output with a minimum of messy detail. We will see more examples of the package's use during the hands-on part of the laboratory. Documentation is available by accessing the file `A:\docs\index.html` with your browser.

Review Questions

1. List the steps in the program development process.

2. How does Java indicate a comment? What are comments for?

3. What Java statement will display your name on the screen?

4. What are the two categories of variable types?

5. What is Java's type name for a whole number value like 2 or -5?

6. What is Java's type name for a number with a decimal point like 2.67?

7. What symbol must come at the end of every Java declaration and statement?

8. What is the type that has only two possible values: true or false?

9. If a Java file is saved under the name Dumb.java, what is the name of the public class contained in that file?

10. Write (using pencil and paper) Java statements that declare a variable with the name bestValue and then give it the initial value of 99.9. We

assume that this variable will be used to store numbers with decimal points.

11. Assuming that the variable in the previous question has been declared, what Java statement will change its value to twice its previous value?

12. What is the Java name for a reference to a block of characters?

13. Write a minimal Java program that displays your name on the screen once and then stops, using the method `System.out.println` (without using a ViewFrame object). Assume that you would save the program in a file called Name.java.

14. Modify the previous program so it uses a ViewFrame object from the LabPkg package.

15. What is a Java package?

16. Find the Web page with documentation on the classes in LabPkg. *Hint:* Start with the page `A:\index.html`.

17. If x is 5 and y is 7, what is the value of the following expression:

    `x != y && !(x < 4 || y < x)`

Projects or Not?[4]

A project is a collection of files that make up a single program. Many IDEs require that the programmer create a project even if the program will be a single file. (The Kawa IDE allows you to create a program that consists of a single file, compile it, and run it without creating a project. This is nice for small assignments that involve only one file.)

Rule: If your program will involve more than a single file, create a new project in the IDE using the `Project>New` menu selection. Then create each file and "add" it to the project.

When you are not actively working with a project, be sure to close it. Projects that are open automatically move to the top of the project list in the Kawa Project frame.

Pre-Laboratory Task

In each of our laboratories we will make use of files that we will modify or simply test. These files are to be transferred from the student diskette that comes with the text to a folder on your hard drive—saving extensive typing on your part. Throughout this lab book we will assume that your working directory is `Z:\lab_files\`. The `Z:` drive could be a removable diskette drive, a high performance removable disk drive such as a Zip disk drive, a network drive, or a local hard drive. Because of these many options, we will agree to simply call the work space `Z:\lab_files\`.

To download files for this laboratory, open your Web browser (Netscape or Internet Explorer) and enter the URL

`file:///A:/index.html`

---

4. Recall that we will be using the Kawa IDE for demonstration. If you have another IDE, refer to Appendix B for how to create a project and add files to it.

(You can directly copy the files from the diskette, but you will not easily figure out which files go with which laboratory. Ask your instructor whether you should copy files directly from the diskette.)

Scroll down until you see the table of laboratories. For this lab, Laboratory 1, click on the "Files to download" link and you will see the page shown below.

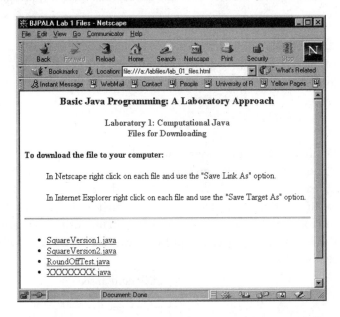

The instructions indicate how to download the files. Be sure you save them in the folder Z:\lab_files\. Once the files have been downloaded, you can proceed to do the required tasks of this lab.

Please note that this same procedure will be completed prior to the start of every laboratory experience.

The Laboratory

Objectives

- To become familiar with the IDE.
- To run and modify some simple programs.
- To write some programs using the LabPkg package.

A Guide to the Laboratory

- Task 1 compiles, runs, and then modifies SquareVersion1.java. There is nothing to turn in.
- Task 2 simply requires that you compile and run SquareVersion2.java to see how one can create an event-driven version of the program. There is nothing to turn in.
- Read the section on "Writing a Program—Guidelines" before starting task 3.
- Task 3 requires the creation of a program "from scratch" that will read in two numbers that represent the length and width of a rectangle and will display the area and the length of the diagonal. You will want to use SquareVersion1.java as a model. You will need to see how some of

the Math methods are used. Turn in a copy of RectData.java when you are finished.

> In this initial laboratory, we will use the Kawa IDE. If you are using another IDE, you will want to keep the appropriate page from Appendix B handy.

Task 1: Using Your IDE to Compile and Run Programs

We will start by opening, compiling, and running a simple program. We will look at a program that reads in a whole number and displays its square on the screen.

Opening a Java Program File

Double-click on the Kawa icon or start the IDE software from the `Start>` `Programs` menu. When the software opens, go to the `File` menu and select `Open` (`File>Open`). When the file finder dialog box pops up, make sure you locate the folder `Z:\lab_files\`. Consider the picture below, which shows the folder on the removable drive `D:` on an author's computer. (Remember that the use of `Z:` is just a convention. Local circumstances will determine what `Z:` really is.)

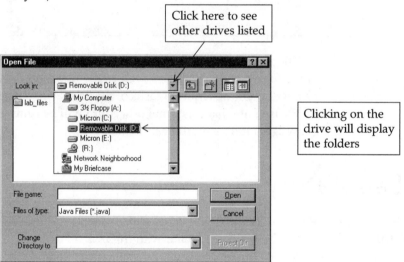

After clicking where shown, scroll until you see the Z: drive (D: in the picture above). Clicking on it shows the folders. Click on the `lab_files` folder. You should see the file `SquareVersion1.java` if you downloaded it properly. Double-click on it to open it in the editing window (shown below).

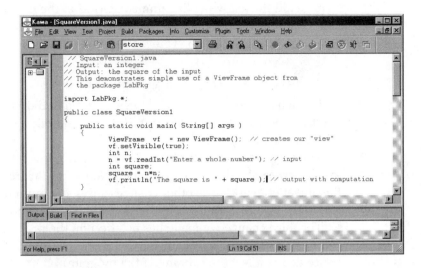

This program occupies only the single file, so a project is not necessary. (If your IDE requires a project, create one with the name `SquareV1` and add this file to it.) We will compile it, then run it.

Compiling

To compile a file, use `Build>Compile` (select the Build menu, then the Compile option) or press the **F7** key along the top of the keyboard. There is also a button on the toolbar for this operation. The actual command to compile is shown in the Build frame at the bottom of the Kawa window. You should see a "No errors" message.

Running

To run a compiled program, use `Build>Run` or press the **F4** key or the special button on the toolbar.

This program has a visual component, which will appear after two to three seconds. (If you don't see it, it may be obscured by the IDE's window. Simply iconify the IDE's window for a moment.) A pop-up dialog will ask you for an integer. Enter the value `-25`, and click "Ok" or simply press the **Enter** key after typing the value. In the output window you should see a message indicating that the square is 625.

The program is finished, but visual components are persistent—they simply won't disappear until you close the window (click on the X in the upper-right corner). We have provided an alternative way to kill the window—a button labelled "Exit." Press it (click on it) and a dialog box will appear and will ask if you really want to quit. Click on the "Yes" button or simply press the **Enter** key as the "Yes" button is highlighted.

Making Modifications

We will show off some additional features of our ViewFrame object that may be useful. In the editing window of the IDE, make the following changes:

- Replace
  ```
  new ViewFrame()
  ```
  with
  ```
  new ViewFrame("SquareVersion1")
  ```
- Before the line with `vf.readInt(...);`, add the following line:
  ```
  vf.setIOEcho(true);
  ```

- Add the following line immediately after the first line of the file. Of course, you should actually put in your name and the name of your lab partner rather than "your name(s)."
  ```
  // your name(s)
  ```
- Save the file, compile it again, and run it.

If you had errors, you probably made a typo or didn't make the changes exactly as described above. Correct them and compile again.

What changed?

You may not have noticed before, but the window has a title. Unless you say otherwise, the title is "ViewFrame." Now it is "SquareVersion1," without the quotation marks. The other change causes any input to also appear (be *echoed*) in the output window. This helps if you make a typo when entering data.

The third change we made has no effect on the program. It was simply a comment containing your name(s). Comments are ignored by the compiler and hence do not affect the running of the program.

If you forget to include

```
vf.setVisible(true);
```

you will have a problem. Let's see what that problem is. Put // in front of that line to comment it out. This means that the computer will ignore the line. Now save, recompile, and run the program.

No window appears except for the pop-up dialog. After entering your number you see nothing. The window still exists—it is just invisible! How do we terminate the window when we can't see it?

Using Kawa, go to the Build menu and select the Stop Run option (`Build>Stop Run`). This can be used to terminate any running program.

An alternative approach to killing a running program (that is independent of the IDE) is to use the Task Manager to terminate the Java interpreter. Right-clicking the icon bar at the bottom of most Windows screens will provide a menu. Select Task Manager and then its Applications tab. You should see the running program listed by its component's name. Highlight it and select End Task.

Rule: After creating a ViewFrame object, be sure to make it visible!

Printing a File

You can now go to the `File` menu and select `Print` to get a copy of the file. This should come out on the printer associated with your computer. You will not have to turn this in, but you need to be sure you know how to print a file.

Closing a File

We have finished with this program, so go to the File menu and select Close (`File>Close`).

Closing a Project

Kawa did not require a project for this example, but if it had you would have needed to close the project. In Kawa this is done by highlighting the project in the project frame list and right-clicking. One of the menu options is Close.

Task 2: Using a Button

We can modify our first version to use a button. You can try it out by opening `SquareVersion2.java`, compiling it, and running it. Don't worry about the details for now! (As usual, if your IDE requires a project, create one in `Z:\lab_files\` called `SquareV2`.)

Of course, you should click on the button labeled "Do it" to cause the computation to start. After it completes, click on the "Do it" button again. This allows us to do the computation as many times as we need to without restarting the program. This makes our example *event-driven* although the only critical event is the clicking on a button.

Close all open files in the IDE. (If your IDE required a project, close it.)

Writing a Program— Guidelines

Creating a Java program requires the following steps:

1. Design your solution and determine how to implement it in Java.

2. If two or more files will be created, you must create a project and then add the files to the project as they are created. The name of the project is not critical but should reflect the nature of the program.

3. For each file to be created, select New on the File menu (`File>New`), enter the code (don't forget comments), and then save the file (`File>Save`). You will be asked where it should be saved and what should be its name. Generally, keep all files for a project in the same folder.

4. Compile the file. For multiple file projects, you may want to compile the entire project. In Kawa this is done with `Build>Rebuild All`.

5. Correct any errors. Error messages are presented with the line number where the error occurred. **You can double-click on the error message's line and go directly to the line in the file where the error occurs.** It is usually only necessary to correct the first error, then recompile. Often other errors may not actually be errors at all, as the first error can confuse the compiler.

6. After all errors have been fixed and the file has been recompiled, run the file.

7. Test the program with various data values, running the program as often as needed. If incorrect results occur, go back and look at your logic to find what went wrong. Fix any logical errors and start again to compile and test.

8. At this point you will either print out the final version to turn in or mail the file(s) as an attachment.

Task 3: A Simple Program Using the Math Operations

The Problem

With your partner write a solution to the following programming problem on a sheet of paper. You should use SquareVersion1.java as a program model.

Problem: Write a program in a file called `RectData.java` that will request that the user enter two integers representing the length and width of a rectangle. The program should then display the area and the length of the diagonal. Be sure that you indicate the meanings of the output values by labeling them, i.e., displaying a message like "The area is . . ."

The formula for the diagonal of a rectangle is

$$diagonal = \sqrt{width^2 + length^2}$$

The Math methods should be used to get the proper value.

Once you think you have the solution, open a new file and begin entering the program. Name your main class `RectData`. When you have finished entering the code, select Save on the File menu (`File>Save`). It should be saved in the same folder as the other files. It should be named `RectData.java`.

Compile the program and fix any errors. Be sure to test your program. Try the input values 3 and 4 to see if the area is 12 and the diagonal is 5.0. Also try 1 and 1. The area should be 1 and the diagonal should be the square root of 2, or approximately 1.414.

Print out a copy of your Java program file `RectData.java` and turn it in with the other items submitted for this lab.

Post-Laboratory Exercises

These exercises are assigned as needed by your instructor. They provide additional practice.

Illustrating Roundoff

Close all files and open the file `RoundOffTest.java`. The main method for the file RoundOffTest.java is shown below:

```java
import LabPkg.*;
public class RoundOffTest
{
    public static void main(String[] args)
    {
        ViewFrame vf = new ViewFrame("Round Off Demo");
        vf.setVisible(true);

        double d;
        d = 9.000000101;
        double root;
        root = Math.sqrt(d);
        vf.println("Square root of " + d +
                " is " + root);
        vf.println("Square of " + root + " is " +
                root * root);
        vf.println("Square of " + root + " is " +
                Math.pow(root, 2.0));
    }
}
```

We have declared two variables, d and root, which are both double. Double means that the variable has decimal points and has *double precision*. The double precision means that it keeps the maximum number of significant digits possible.

Notice that we are squaring the square root of d two different ways. Will the results equal d? Perhaps not. This could be because of roundoff in taking the square root or in the product computation.

Compile and run the program. Notice that the square of the square root of d *almost* equals d. Replace 9.000000101 with 231.56005 and remake the project. Then run it. This works.

What is the point? It doesn't always work due to roundoff!

Your Task

Try to find a value other than 9.000000101 that the square of its square root fails to equal it. Do this by modifying the program above so you enter the value for d at the keyboard. You will need to use `vf.readDouble("Enter a number")`. Now you can run the program several times without remaking it.

Print out the modified program and write on it the value you found. Make sure your name is on it and turn it in.

Practice Exercises

These are relatively short exercises for practice. Model them on SquareVersion1.java.

1. Write a program in a file called `Sqrt.java` that will ask for a positive integer and display its square root.

2. Write a program in a file called `Average.java` that will ask for two numbers and display their average. The average is the sum of the values divided by `2.0`.

3. Write a program called `GeometricMean.java` that will read in two positive values and display their geometric mean. The geometric mean of two values is the square root of their product.

Challenge Exercise: Computing Your Loan Payments

If you wish to borrow money at simple interest for a car, you will make monthly payments for 36 or 48 months, in most cases. Because you must pay interest each month on the remaining balance and that interest is taken directly from the current payment before the payment is applied to reducing the loan, computing the payment amount requires some sophisticated algebra.

We could derive the formula, but we will simply state it after defining the variables.

```
annual_rate // a double precision value like 0.065 for 6.5%
rate        // simply annual_rate / 12.0
principal   // the amount borrowed, like 16500.0 for $16,500
n           // an integer like 36 representing the number
            // of monthly payments
payment     // the amount to be paid each month, like 268.95
```

Notice that all the values except for n are doubles. Be careful to note that `annual_rate` is not a percentage, but is the decimal value found by dividing the percentage by 100.

The formula is

$$payment = \frac{principal \cdot \left(1 - \frac{1}{1 + rate}\right)}{\frac{1}{1 + rate} - \left(\frac{1}{1 + rate}\right)^{n + 1}}$$

You may want to evaluate $\frac{1}{1 + rate}$ first as a quantity T, and use T in the formula.

Why? The problem with our formula is that in Java we must write it on a single line. For example, the simple expression $\frac{1}{1 + rate}$ must be written as 1/(1+*rate*). Lots of parentheses are needed, but the right-hand side is not too bad if we use

```
double T = 1 / (1 + rate);
double payment = principal * (1 - T) / (T - Math.pow(T, n + 1));
```

Loan.java

Write a Java program `Loan.java` that will request the amount to be borrowed, the *annual* interest rate as a decimal like .065, and the number of monthly payments. It then should display the monthly payment computed using the formula above but to two decimal places, i.e., in dollars and cents form. It should use the LabPkg package and use a ViewFrame for output.

Try it with a loan amount equal to 16500.0, an annual rate equal to .065, and a number of payments equal to 36. You should get 505.708547 . . .

If you want the payment to be rounded to two decimal places, consider the following assignment:

```
payment = Math.round(payment * 100) / 100.0;
```

Can you see why this works?

Of course, your bank will not round, but will use the "ceiling" method. When using `Math.ceil()`, any fractional part to the right of the decimal that is not 0 causes the result to be the next highest integer. So `Math.ceil(2.0000001)` is `3.0`. Use the ceiling method (instead of the round method) to display the payment to two decimal places.

After testing your program, print out a copy of Loan.java to turn in. Be sure your name is in a comment.

Questions

Use your program to answer the following questions. Put the answers on your printout.

1. If you borrow $20,000 to buy a car for four years (48 payments) at 7.5% annual interest, what is your monthly payment?

2. What is the payment if you can find a rate of 6%?

3. What would be the payment if you borrowed at 7.5%, but for three years instead of four?

Another Challenge Exercise (optional)

The `Loan.java` program would be nicer if we could run it several times by simply clicking on a button. Create a file `LoanWithButton.java` that will have a button labeled "Compute Loan Payment" that when pressed will collect the data about the loan and then display the monthly payment in the ViewFrame object's output area.

This is easier if you start with the template file `XXXXXXXX.java` and use the editor to do a replacement of all occurrences of "XXXXXXXX" (eight capital Xs) with the text "LoanWithButton" and then Save As to name the file `LoanWithButton.java`. Now the model of `SquareVersion2.java` and the computation of `Loan.java` should be enough to get this working.

2

Leap Years

In the previous laboratory we examined programs that did simple computation. The programs were sequential, i.e., they performed all the instructions in the order they were listed in the main method. In this lab we will use a facility provided by all programming languages—the selection or choice of which instructions to execute based on conditions that are true or false. For example, if it were true that a value x was not 0, then we could execute an instruction that involved division by x. However, if x were 0, then a different set of instructions would have to be executed or the program would maybe even terminate. In Java these choices or selections are implemented using if statements.

Pre-Laboratory Reading

Boolean Expressions

Java has two special values: `true` and `false`. These are considered constants. They are the only values possible for boolean expressions. **By definition, a boolean expression is an expression that has either the value true or the value false.**

The usual comparison operators used for numbers in algebra are available:

```
x < y            true if x is less than y
x == y           true if x equals y
x != y           true if x is not equal to y
x <= y           true if x less than or equal to y
x > y            true if x is greater than y
x >= y           true if x is greater than or equal to y
```

In the examples above, we assume x and y are numeric values. If an expression is not true, then it must be false. Take note of how we ask about equality—two equal signs! This avoids confusion with assignment expressions, which have a single equal sign.

Boolean Operators— "and," "or," and "not"

Boolean expressions can be combined by using the operators `&&` (meaning "and"), `||` (meaning "or"), and `!` (meaning "not"). The `&&` has higher precedence than the `||`. The `!` operation has the highest precedence (without parentheses).

The "and" of two boolean expressions is true only if *both* expressions are true. The "or" of two boolean expressions is true provided *either* one is true *or* both are true. "Not" simply changes the truth value to its opposite.

In Java, the mathematical inequality $3 < x \le 10$ is true for a value of x if the boolean expression

```
3 < x && x <= 10
```

is true. Notice that we must repeat the x. The mathematical expression is shorthand for saying x is greater than 3 *and* x is less than or equal to 10.

Selection Statements in Java—"if" and "if-else"

The "if" statement uses a boolean condition to determine whether or not to perform certain statements. It comes in two forms.

Simple "if"

```
if ( boolean condition )
      statement
```

The boolean condition is evaluated. If it is true, then the statement is executed. Otherwise, the statement is skipped and ignored.

"if-else"

```
if ( boolean condition )
      statement1
else
      statement2
```

The boolean condition is evaluated. If it is true, then statement1 is executed. If it is false, statement2 is executed. Only one of the statements is executed. The other is skipped.

Example 1

```
if (x < 0)
    System.out.println("Sorry, negative value");
else
    System.out.println("Square root is " + Math.sqrt(x));
```

This is a very simple example using the if-else form. Since we cannot take the square root of a negative value, it makes sense to check for that condition. Notice that if x < 0 is false, then x is greater than or equal to 0 and we can take its square root. Only one of the two statements will be done, and it depends entirely on the condition (and hence the value of x) as to which is executed.

Example 2

```
if (n == 0)
{
    System.out.println("Zero encountered. Terminating program!");
    System.exit(1);   // stop program immediately
}
```

This is an example of a *simple if*, but we have used a *compound statement*. We wanted to do two statements if n == 0 was true. The syntax only allows one statement! Java (and most other languages) has a simple fix—it allows multiple statements to be grouped together and count as a unit. Java uses the *curly braces* for this.

```
{
    statement
    statement
    ...
    statement
}
```

Compound statements have another special feature—unlike assignment statements they are never followed by a semicolon. The closing brace makes it unnecessary.

Finally, we need to make special mention of the method exit() in the System class. System.exit(1) and System.exit(0) both terminate the program immediately. By convention, the 0 value means nothing was wrong, while the 1 value means an error of some kind occurred. This is a rather severe action and often the displayed message is not seen if it is part of a visual component created by the program!

Review Questions

1. If x is an integer variable that has been declared and given a value, what Java statement will print "Zero" if it has the value 0 and "Not Zero" otherwise? Use System.out.println("...") for displaying the message.

2. Suppose x and y are two integer variables that have been declared and given values. Write a Java statement that will display the larger of the two values (without using Math.max()). Do not worry about whether they may be equal in value.

Multiple Options— The if-else-if-else Pattern

Consider this case: a user enters an integer value that represents a test grade. Suppose the value is stored in the variable called grade. If the grading system is of the form

```
90 and above is an A
80-89 is a B
70-79 is a C
```

```
60-69 is a D
below 60 is a F
```

we could write the following code to display the letter grade:

```java
if (grade >= 90)
{
   System.out.println("A");
}
else
{
   if (grade >= 80 && grade < 90)
   {
       System.out.println("B");
   }
   else
   {
       if (grade >= 70 && grade < 80)
       {
           System.out.println("C");
       }
       else
       {
           if (grade >= 60 && grade < 70)
           {
               System.out.println("D");
           }
           else
           {
               System.out.println("F");
           }
       }
   }
}
```

This shows that a statement that is the object of an if condition can itself be another if or if-else statement. Carefully connect the corresponding opening and closing braces to see the structure.

This is correct, but the indentation is somewhat annoying. We essentially are handling multiple options, where only one is true. In such a case we can shorten the code using the style shown below.

```java
if (grade >= 90)
{
   System.out.println("A");
}
else if (grade >= 80 && grade < 90)
{
   System.out.println("B");
}
else if (grade >= 70 && grade < 80)
{
   System.out.println("C");
}
else if (grade >= 60 && grade < 70)
{
   System.out.println("D");
}
else
{
   System.out.println("F");
}
```

Notice how much more readable this form is. This is our choice when we have more than two options. Notice that the last option is simply an else with no condition. This option is automatically done if no previous conditions are true.

In this form only the *first* true condition has its statement(s) executed.

Leap Year Defined

The following was a feature of the University of Kansas' online news.[1] It was taken from the Web page located at `http://www.ur.ku.edu/News/96N/FebNews/Feb20/leapyear.html`. It is dated February 20, 1996.

SO YOU THOUGHT LEAP YEAR CAME EVERY FOUR YEARS!

Lawrence, Kansas - Leap year doesn't come every four years—not always.

True, 1996 is a leap year, and so we add a day to February. The year 2000, a century year, will be a leap year, too. But if every fourth year were a leap year, our calendars and our seasons would gradually grow apart, said Barbara Anthony-Twarog, professor of physics and astronomy at the University of Kansas.

So some years aren't leap years although they're divisible by four. Anthony-Twarog explains why.

Leap years are needed to bring together our two methods of calculating the length of a year. One measure is the time the earth takes to complete an orbit around the sun. The other is the number of days, or Earth rotations, in that period, Anthony-Twarog said.

More than 2,000 years ago, astronomers knew that the difference between the two methods of calculating is about a quarter of a day. They figured the orbital year at 365.2422 days by noting the interval between vernal equinoxes. The vernal equinox occurs in the spring, around March 21.

The Julian calendar, produced by Julius Caesar, added a day every four years to account for that leftover fraction of a day, Anthony-Twarog said. This calendar worked well for a while, but by the late 16th century, when the calendar read March 21, spring was lagging two weeks behind, according to the sun's position and the weather.

In the late 16th century Pope Gregory XIII commanded radical calendar reform to avert further embarrassment. The Gregorian plan went into effect in 1582 in the Roman Catholic countries of Europe, but not without some pain, Anthony-Twarog said.

Ten days were dropped from the calendar—in October of that year—to adjust matters. How would you feel if someone dropped 10 days out of a month but still charged you for a full month's rent?

Protestant governments and countries obedient to the Eastern Rite churches ignored the mandate. England and its colonies held out until 1752, and Russia didn't alter its calendar until 1917, Anthony-Twarog said.

How does the Gregorian calendar work? Knowing that the year must be 365.2422 days long, the first step is to keep the scheme of adding a day every fourth year. That makes the average year 365.25 days long—a bit too long.

Removing one leap-day per century brings the calendar down to 365.2400 days, so century years are generally not leap years. Adding back century years divisible by 400 makes the year length 365.2425 days long, close enough to the Earth's orbital period that the error is less than one day in 3,300 years. So the year 2000 will be a leap year. The next century year that will be a leap year is 2400.

Selecting Proper Code—A Paper and Pencil Exercise

Using the if Statement to Check for Leap Years

We might want to write a program that will determine if a year typed in at the keyboard is a leap year based on the following definition:

> A year in the current calendar system, i.e., after 1582, is a leap year if it is divisible by 4, with the exception that if it is divisible by 100 but not by 400, it is not a leap year.

So 1933 is not a leap year, but 1960 is a leap year. 1700 is not a leap year, but 1600 is a leap year. Keep the examples in mind as you do the rest of the lab. (Note that if a year can be divided by 100 it can be divided by 4. Similarly, any year that can be divided by 400 can be divided by 100 and by 4.)

In practice, the year should be at least 1582. (Why?) However, we will not check for this in the code that we will be examining.

Divisible By...

When one has two integers, A and B, and B is not 0, then A *is divisible by* B if A%B is 0. For example, a number is *even* provided it is divisible by 2. In Java we might write

```
if (x % 2 == 0) // is x even?
   System.out.println("Even");
else
   System.out.println("Odd");
```

What Works?

For each of the following options, A, B, C, and D, you will see statements that are part of a Java program. Assume that the variable year was given a value that was entered by a user. Assume that it was checked to see that it was positive and greater than 1582. Read each option carefully. There should be no syntax errors.

Determine which options correctly determine if the year is a leap year and print the appropriate message.

You should try some values and check them by *tracing*. Tracing is the method of simulating the actions of the computer with paper and pencil.

At least one is incorrect, and at least one is correct. Which are they? For the one(s) with incorrect results, indicate a year for which the code doesn't work properly.

Option A

```
if (year % 4 == 0 && year % 400 == 0) {
   System.out.println("It's a leap year!");
}
else {
   System.out.println("It's NOT a leap year.");
}
```

Option B

```
if (year % 4 != 0) {
   System.out.println("It's NOT a leap year.");
}
else {
   if (year % 100 == 0){
       System.out.println("It's NOT a leap year.");
   }
   else {
       System.out.println("It's a leap year!");
   }
}
```

Option C

```
if (year % 400 == 0) {
```

```
                              System.out.println("It's a leap year!");
                          }
                          else if (year % 100 == 0) {
                              System.out.println("It's NOT a leap year.");
                          }
                          else if (year % 4 == 0) {
                              System.out.println("It's a leap year!");
                          }
                          else {
                              System.out.println("It's NOT a leap year.");
                          }
```

Option D
```
                          if (year % 4 != 0) {
                              System.out.println("It's NOT a leap year.");
                          }
                          else {
                              if (year % 100 == 0 && year % 400 != 0) {
                                  System.out.println("It's NOT a leap year.");
                              }
                              else {
                                  System.out.println("It's a leap year!");
                              }
                          }
```

The Laboratory

Objectives

- To successfully write simple programs that involve if statements.
- To gain practice in the use of boolean operators like && and ||.

A Guide to the Laboratory

- Task 1 requires that you take the program RectData.java that you wrote in the previous lab and modify it to avoid non-positive values. Turn in a printout of the modified program.
- Task 2 requires that you write a complete program Options.java that will accept an integer as input and display one of these messages: "positive," "negative," or "zero." When this program is working properly, print out a copy to turn in.
- Task 3 requires that you write a complete program Big3.java to read in three integers and display the largest value without using any of the Math methods. Turn in a printout of your solution.

Preliminaries

There are no files to download for this laboratory.

Task 1: Avoiding Bad Input

The program RectData.java reads in two numbers that represent the length and width of a rectangle. In the previous lab, we didn't check if the numbers were 0 or negative values, which wouldn't be meaningful.

Open RectData.java in the IDE and modify it to check for 0 and negative values of the two numbers that are entered. Do the computation only if both values are positive. Otherwise, execute the statement

```
vf.println("Bad input");
```

if you used a ViewFrame object called vf in your program.

Print out a copy of the revised program to turn in. Be sure to include your name(s) in a comment. If you have changed lab partners, use the current names.

Task 2: Multiple Options

Write a new program called Options.java that will request that the user enter an integer and then will display the message "positive," "negative," or "zero" if the value that was entered was greater than zero, less than zero, or equal to zero, respectively.

Turn in a printout with your name(s) on it.

Task 3: Finding the Largest Value

It is easy to find the largest of two values and print it out using an if statement. For example, if a and b are the values, then

```
if (a > b)
    System.out.println("" + a);
else
    System.out.println("" + b);
```

will work. (Of course, we may want to display the answer using a visual component such as a ViewFrame object and its println() method, but that is a simple modification.)

You are to create a new program in the file Big3.java that will request three integers from the user and display the largest of the values. Do *not* use the method Math.max(). Use a ViewFrame object to obtain input and display the answer.

Turn in a printout of your program with your name(s) on it when the program is working properly. Be sure to test it with all possible orders of three numbers.

Post-Laboratory Exercises

Acid or Alkaline?

Write a program called PH.java that will accept a value with a decimal point from the user. If the value is 0 or negative or if it is greater than 12.0, display a message indicating bad data. Otherwise, if the value entered is less than 6.0, display the message "acidic." If it is greater than 6.0, display the message "alkaline." If it equals 6.0, display the message "neutral."

Quotients

Write a program in a file called Quotients.java that will read in two integers from the user. If either integer is negative, replace it by its absolute value. If either integer is 0, display the message "No quotient." Otherwise, display the quotient of the larger value divided by the smaller value.

Leap Year

Select the leap year code option that you felt was correct from options A through D and write a complete program LeapYear.java to test it.

Warning Messages

LabPkg's ViewFrame has a useful method `showWarningMsg` that will display a warning message that will not go away until dismissed by the user. It solves the problem of killing the program before the user can read the message. For example, if `vf` is a ViewFrame object, then

```
if (n == 0)
{
    vf.showWarningMsg("Zero value encountered - quitting");
    System.exit(1);
}
```

will allow the user to read the message before the ViewFrame window disappears due to the execution of System.exit(1).

3

Object-Oriented Java

In this lab we want to explore Java's features as an object-oriented language. Our initial focus will be on graphical objects. Java provides a large collection of classes that support graphics, and it is relatively easy to use them.

The pre-laboratory reading will discuss the main features of object-oriented programming.

Pre-Laboratory Reading

Concepts

Object-oriented programming requires the programmer to view programs differently from the older procedural programming paradigm. It also requires a language that supports classes and objects. Both Java and C++ can be used for object-oriented programming. Object-oriented programming has been promoted as a more productive and natural way to view solutions to problems. Object-oriented programmers are more productive because the classes they create for one project may be reusable on another project. It is a natural way of viewing software development, because many problems are stated in terms of objects which then interact. The interaction is what causes the computation to progress.

The object-oriented paradigm requires that we examine the following concepts:

- classes, objects, and the creation process
- packages
- public
- methods
- data members or "fields"
- static methods and static data members
- extending a class to get a new class
- a class that implements an interface
- container classes
- a class hierarchy

This will be a whirlwind look at a very sophisticated topic. Don't worry if it doesn't all make sense. The entire course will be spent learning more about each part.

Classes, Objects, and the Creation Process

- An object is said to be an "instance" of a class.
- A class is a model for objects.

This is not very informative, so let's consider what an object is.

An object is a programming entity that has data components representing the current state of the object and methods[1] that allow the other programming entities to interact with it. For example, in a program that performed a traffic simulation at a busy intersection, one type of object would be a car. The car *class* would describe all car objects by indicating what data components each would have and what methods each would have. The data components maybe would include current position, current velocity, and type of car. Each object would have an area of memory set aside for its values for these data components. Typical methods would maybe set a new velocity for the car, allow other objects to obtain the current position or the type of the car, and destroy the car object to remove it from the simulation.

Every class provides a special method that is called when an object is initially created. This is called a *constructor method*, and usually provides special initialization of data components. There can be more than one constructor

---

1. Informally, a method is defined as a named collection of instructions. See the next page for more information.

method for a class, each distinguishable from the others by the data it requires in order to construct the object. This data is supplied in the form of a *parameter list*, described below.

Packages

A package is a collection of classes. All of the files in the same folder as the current program have their classes as part of the "default" package. The "import" directive in Java is used to tell the current program of other packages that are available and are not found in the current folder.

public

The adjective "public" is often associated with classes and their methods. It means that other classes and methods can use them without being part of the same package.

Java requires that a file contain exactly one public class. Other classes may be defined in the file but may not be designated as public.

Methods

Methods are named collections of instructions. Much of the work of a program is performed by making calls to methods, either ones that are provided with the language (e.g., `Math.sqrt()`) or ones that you or other programmers have written. Methods have the following basic syntax:

```
adjectives return_type NAME( parameter_list )
{
    instructions are here
}
```

The adjectives can be "public/private/protected" and "static," all of which can be omitted.

The `return_type` is either `void` or a primitive type (int, double, char, and so on) or a reference to an object (String, ViewFrame, Canvas, and so on). **It cannot be omitted.** If the return type is void, we call the method a *procedure,* and otherwise call it a *function.* Functions must have the special instruction

```
return expression;
```

among their instructions, where the value of `expression` has the type of what is to be returned.

If a car object named `x` had a method `setSpeed`, then it would be "called" in the following manner:

```
x.setSpeed(35);
```

The effect would be to change the speed data component of `x` to 35. This is a *procedure.* We think of `x.setSpeed(35)` as a short name for the instructions in `setSpeed`.

An example of a *function* associated with a car object might be a method getSpeed which would provide the current value of the speed data component for the object. It could be used as follows:

```
int s;
s = x.getSpeed();
if (s == 0) // x is stopped
...
```

Methods are recognized by a name followed by parentheses. Values may be put in the parentheses or not, depending upon the method's definition.

`parameter_list` is optional. If it appears, it specifies data that is provided for use by the method. For example, the method `setSpeed` of the car class could be defined as follows:

```
public void setSpeed(int s)
{
    ...
}
```

The parameter list would consist of only the single parameter s, which would be the new speed. All listed parameters must have their type declared. If more than one parameter is listed, each is separated from the others by commas.

Data Members or "Fields"

Data members are variables associated with a particular object. They are declared just as normal variables are, except they can be designated as public, private, or protected. If x were an object and p were a public data member, then x.p could be used to refer to the object. If the data member p was private or protected, then x.p would not be legal, and the normal access to p's value would be via a method of x, if access were required.

Static

If a method or data member is static, then it can be referred to by

`classname.datamembername`

This allows you to refer to a data member or use a method without creating an object. A good example is the Math class. The method sqrt is static, so it can be used as Math.sqrt(5.6). The Math class also has a public static data member, PI, a double value that estimates pi, the ratio of the circumference of a circle to its diameter. Any Java program that needs to use the value pi can do so by referring to Math.PI.

A special method is always static—main. Recall that execution of a program starts with the first instruction in main. If main were not static, then it could not be called before the creation of an object; but that would require an instruction prior to calling main.

We now can see all of the key parts of main's definition.

```
public static void main(String[] args)
{
    ... instructions
}
```

main must be public and static so it can be called to start a program. It performs actions and has no return statement, so its return type is void. It has one parameter, args, of type String[]. In most applications this parameter is not used, but it is still required in the definition.

Extending a Class

It is quite common for a programmer to have defined a nice class and then later, when writing some other program, realize that a specialized version of that class with some additional capabilities is needed. Rather than redefining the entire class to get the new version, the programmer can "extend" the class and add the new features. All the methods and data components of the original class are automatically available. The programmer adds the new data components or the new methods. If an existing method needs changing, it is just rewritten. The methods that are not rewritten are unaffected.

Consider a class MotorVehicle that has general data components and methods for motor vehicles used in a traffic simulation. It would be natural to have specialized versions like Car or Truck or Motorcycle. Java allows this by adding "extends *classname*" in the declaration of the specialized class. For example,

```
public class Truck extends MotorVehicle
```

automatically says that `Truck` can have access to all `MotorVehicle` data that is not private. Protected and public data components are automatically available to the extensions of a class, but private data components are not. Think of protected data as sharable within the family, public data as sharable with anyone, and private data as not sharable at all.

The big advantage of this concept is that we can extend a class provided by Java in one of its many packages. Our extension can be simple, and we can use all of the methods and data that come with the original class. We will see this done in this laboratory and study it extensively in later labs.

Implementing

An *interface* in Java is a listing of methods. A class is said to *implement* the interface if it contains all of the methods of the interface. Of course, it can have additional methods. For example, the Runnable interface lists only one method,

`public void run()`

so any class that contains the method `run` is said to implement Runnable.

The purpose of an interface is to specify the behavior of an object by specifying what methods it must support. We shall see how useful this can be in a later laboratory.

Containers

Some classes are designed primarily to hold many data values that are objects. These are often called *container* classes. Java provides a Vector class, which maintains a list of objects in linear order. The class Frame is part of the java.awt package and appears as a window with a border. It can contain other visible objects like Panels, Buttons, Canvases, and so on. Container classes always organize the objects they contain in some designated way. Graphical container classes like Frame maintain a layout of their visible components so that when the window is resized, the components are properly repositioned.

Class Hierarchy

The ability to create specialized versions of classes using the "extends" concept and keyword automatically creates a hierarchy of classes. At the top of every class hierarchy is the Object class. The diagram below gives a listing of some classes in the hierarchy used for graphical components. The Component class is

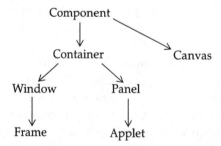

the top of the hierarchy and is a special case of an `Object`. Its objects are visible graphical entities. A `Canvas` is a special extension of a `Component`. It allows drawing and image displays but cannot contain or display other visual components. `Container` extends `Component`; both `Window` and `Panel` extend `Container`. At each level of the hierarchy, each class extends the class above it and inherits all of the methods of the class that it extends. So `Frame` inherits all the methods from `Window`, which inherits all the methods from `Container`, which inherits all the methods from `Component`.

If we were to write a class that extends `Frame`, we could automatically have access to all the methods of `Frame` and its ancestors in the hierarchy!

Form of a Class Definition

Classes have four parts:

- data components—variables
- constructor methods
- other methods
- (optional) inner classes

The inner classes are classes that can be used only within this class. They have access to the data components and methods of the class.

A Person Class

We could define a class with objects that represented individuals and with data components that consisted of the individuals' names and dates of birth. The class might be defined as follows:

```
public class Person
{
    private String name;
    private String dob;    // date of birth

    // constructor - performs initialization
    public Person(String n, String d)
    {
        name = n;
        dob = d;
    }

    // method to change the name
    public void setName(String n)
    {
        name = n;
    }

    // method to access the name
    public String getName()
    {
        return name;
    }
}
```

There are no inner classes defined in this example. An object would be declared and created using the "new" operation.

```
Person p = new Person("Jane Austen", "December 16, 1775");
```

The `new` operation calls the constructor and creates a reference to an object with the given name and date of birth. The statement

```
System.out.println(p.getName());
```

would display the name on the screen.

How to Find Out about Existing Classes and Their Methods

Java comes with a large collection of prewritten classes gathered into various packages. Information on all of these is provided on the Web. A link to the Sun Microsystems documentation on Java classes may be found on the Web page

`file:///A:/index.html`

located on the diskette that accompanies this text.

The documentation is organized by packages. `Java.lang` contains the basic class information concerning the core classes like `Math` and `String`. `Java.awt` and `javax.swing` contain most of the classes used in graphics.

The swing classes were added in version 1.2 to provide a richer collection of visual components.

Before the lab starts, be sure you can answer questions like the ones below using the online documentation.

1. Find the `Frame` class documentation in the package `java.awt`. What methods are defined by `Frame` and which ones are inherited from `Window`?

2. Find the `Math` class in `java.lang`. All the methods are static. What does the documentation say about the `random` method?

3. Find the `Random` class in `java.util`. What are the key methods?

The Laboratory

Objectives

- To become familiar with classes that represent entities that can interact with the user.
- To construct a class that represents a simple ATM (automatic teller machine).

A Guide to the Laboratory

- Your first task is to create a project containing the files `Converters.java` and `CurrencyConverter.java` and compile and run the program. Take a few minutes to try to identify the key parts. There is nothing to turn in at this point.

- Task 2 requires that you modify `CurrencyConverter.java` and test the modifications. Print out and turn in the modified version of CurrencyConverter.java.

- After you close the previous project, task 3 has you create a new project and complete the file `ATM.java` according to step-by-step instructions. This takes some time, so read the instructions carefully. When finished, print out a copy of ATM.java to turn in.

Preliminaries

As usual, open the Web page

`file:///A:/index.html`

in your browser after inserting the diskette that accompanies this textbook. Follow the link to the files for this lab. Download the files to your folder `Z:\lab_files\` or a subfolder that you create for this laboratory.

Task 1: An Example— Currency Converter Objects

It is often useful to be able to convert between two currencies. We will create a class with objects that are specific currency converters. When created, these objects will be given the names of two currencies and the conversion factor that is used. The actual arithmetic is simple. Of course, we would like to have a visual form for our converter, so each instance will have its own ViewFrame object like the one shown below. This particular converter was created to convert between U.S. dollars and Italian lira.

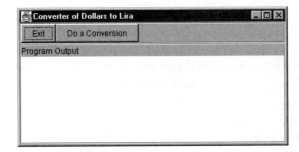

The ViewFrame has a button that initiates a conversion. When it is pressed (i.e., clicked on with the mouse), the user is asked for the number of dollars to convert to lira. After the number of dollars is entered, the result of the conversion appears in the message window. Many conversions can be performed. The Exit button terminates the program.

Notice that the title bar indicates which currencies are involved.

Program Structure

We have two files for this program, so a project should be set up. (Refer to Appendix B for how to create a project if you are using an IDE other than Kawa.)

- Open the IDE and close any open project.
- On the `Project` menu, select `New` (`Project>New`) and create the project in the folder for this lab using the name `CurrencyConversion`. (The Kawa IDE requires that files for a project be in the same folder as the project file itself to run properly.)
- Now on the `Project` menu use the `Add Files` option to add the two files `Converters.java` and `CurrencyConverter.java` to the project.

In the Project frame on the left side of the Kawa window you should see the project listed with its two files. The program is structured as two classes in two separate files. Only one has the main method, while the other defines the CurrencyConverter class and uses an inner class.

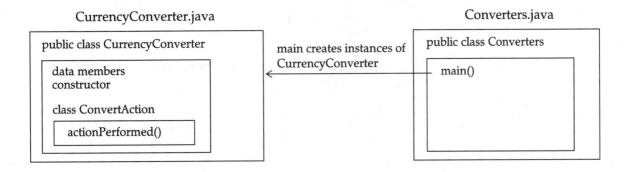

The core of `Converters.java` is simple.

```
public class Converters
{

  public static void main(String[] args)
  {
    new CurrencyConverter("Dollars", "Lira", 1856.8);
    new CurrencyConverter("Lira", "Dollars", 1.0 / 1856.8);
```

```
//new CurrencyConverter("Canadian Dollars", "U.S. Dollars", 1 / 1.467);
    //new CurrencyConverter("Dollars", "French Francs", 6.31);
    //new CurrencyConverter("French Francs", "Dollars", 0.158);
  }
}
```

The current main method creates two objects:

- a converter from dollars to lira
- a converter of lira to dollars

The three commented-out lines show how other converters would be created. Where is the work?

All the work in the program is done by the objects. The program creates objects and lets them interact with each other or the user. This is the essence of object-oriented programming.

Compiling and Running the Program

Compile all the project files. (In Kawa, select Build>Rebuild All or press Shift + F7.)

There should be no errors, so when compilation is completed, run the program. (In Kawa, select Build>Run or press F4.)

Warning: You will see only one window at the upper-left corner of the screen. Actually, there are two windows located at the same spot and one hides the other from view. Use the mouse to move the top window to the right and allow the other window to appear.

You should try a couple of conversions before exiting the application.

Now open the file Converters.java and uncomment the three lines in the main method. Rebuild all the files and re-run the program. You should see five windows—each an instance of the CurrencyConverter class—once you move the windows with the mouse.

Test, then exit the application. In the post-laboratory section you will see how to set the location of windows so they are not all at the same place.

CurrencyConverter Up Close

Open the file CurrencyConverter.java and print a copy to write notes on. The class CurrencyConverter has three parts:

- private data components

```
// data components
private double conversionConstant = 1.0;
private String sourceCurrencyName;
private String targetCurrencyName;
private ViewFrame vf;
```

- a *constructor* method that creates a ViewFrame object and assigns values to the data components

```
// constructor method
public CurrencyConverter(String source, // name of starting currency
                         String target, // name of converted currency
                         double c)       // multiplier to do conversion
{
    sourceCurrencyName = source;
    targetCurrencyName = target;
    conversionConstant = c;
    String msg = "Converter of " + sourceCurrencyName + " to "
                 + targetCurrencyName;
    vf = new ViewFrame(msg);
    // add an action button
    vf.addActionButton(new ConvertAction("Do a Conversion"));
    // this sets the size to be only half as big vertically
    // as the default
    vf.setSize(ViewFrame.WIDTH, ViewFrame.HEIGHT / 2);
```

```
        vf.setVisible(true);
}
```

- an inner class that is an *action* class

```
class ConvertAction extends AbstractAction
{
    // simple constructor required
    public ConvertAction(String s)
    {
        super(s); // sets up button label in AbstractAction
    }

    // the method called when the associated JButton is clicked
    public void actionPerformed(ActionEvent e)
    {
        int amount = vf.readInt("Enter the number of "
                             + sourceCurrencyName);
        double d = amount * conversionConstant;
        vf.println(amount + " " + sourceCurrencyName
                       + " equals " + d + " "
                       + targetCurrencyName);
    }
}// end of ConvertAction class
```

The inner class is just like any other class except it is defined *inside* an enclosing class *but not inside a method*. By being defined there, it has full access to the data components of its enclosing class, but is not accessible to classes other than CurrencyConverter. It really needs access to only the ViewFrame object so it can interact with the user using this ViewFrame object.

Except for the layout of the ViewFrame object, which is handled in the constructor, all of the work is done in the method `actionPerformed()`, which is called automatically when the button is pressed. This is shown in bold. It requests an amount from the user, does the arithmetic, and then displays the answer neatly.

Task 2: Questions and Actions

Answer the following questions *and* modify CurrencyConverter.java to try out your answers:

1. How would you change the label on the conversion button to "CONVERT" instead of "Do a Conversion"?

2. How would you modify the code so that the user could enter a floating point value like 210.75 rather than a whole number when starting a conversion?

3. How would you modify the code so that after the user entered the amount to convert, the program would not do a conversion for a negative value? If a negative were entered, the program would execute the instruction

   `vf.showWarningMsg("Negative values not allowed.");`

   and take no further action. If a non-negative were entered, the conversion would be done and displayed as usual. (**Note:** This requires use of an if-else statement. Look in the previous laboratory for a reminder of how this works.)

Once these questions have been answered and implemented, print out a copy of your modified CurrencyConverter.java and turn it in. Be sure to put your name and the name of your lab partner on it. Close the current project.

Task 3: ATMs

You are to create a new project that will have two files:

- `ATMCreater.java`, with a main method that creates ATM objects
- `ATM.java`, a class that simulates an automated teller machine (ATM)

It is similar in format to the currency conversion example.

Getting Started

First create a project called `ATM_Project` and add the file `ATMCreater.java` to it. `ATMCreater.java` is complete and need not be modified.

Now add the file `ATM.java` to the project. It is partially complete and requires some additions. The file is shown below, with the places for additions marked with boxes.

```
// ATM.java
// Programmers: [                                            ]
//
// Description: Simulates an automated teller machine, but just the
// aspect. It is initiated with a certain number of $20 and $5 bills.
import java.awt.*;
import java.awt.event.*;
import javax.swing.*;
import LabPkg.*;

public class ATM
{

    ViewFrame vf;

    [                                                        ]


    public ATM(int t, int f) // # of $20 and $5 bills to start with
    {
        vf = new ViewFrame("ATM Machine");
        vf.addActionButton(new GeneralButton("Withdrawal"));
        //vf.setIOEcho(true);
        vf.setVisible(true);

        [                                                    ]


    }

    /////////////////////////////////////////////////////
    ////////////////// inner class for a button /////////
    /////////////////////////////////////////////////////
    public class GeneralButton extends AbstractAction
    {
        public GeneralButton(String s)
        {
            super(s);
        }

        public void actionPerformed(ActionEvent e)
        {
            // action when button is pressed goes here

            [                                              ]


        }
```

```
      }

}
```

The inner class, which represents the button, is called `GeneralButton`. This shows that the name is not important provided it is used consistently within the program. In the `CurrencyConverter.java` file, the button class is called `ConvertButton`.

We do need to provide some specifications.

Specifications

First, the constructor will be given two non-negative integers representing the number of $20 bills and the number of $5 bills available in the machine when it starts up. The creation in ATMCreator.java looks like

```
new ATM(30, 40); // 30 $20 bills,  40 $5 bills
```

The constructor indicates the values by the two parameters `t` and `f`. (Look at the file `ATM.java` and find the constructor.) In the example above, `t` would get 30 and `f` would get 40. If the constructor were to get a negative value for a parameter, it should use 0 as the value.

Please note that the two values `t` and `f` in the constructor will not be remembered after the creation process is over unless they are assigned to data members for the object. We suggest declaring two data members, `twenties` and `fives`, which will be used to record the current number of $20 and $5 bills available, respectively.

This ATM is simple because we don't ask for account number and PIN (personal identification number) and only do withdrawals. We simulate the withdrawal of funds, decreasing the number of $20 and $5 bills as the simulation progresses.

The ATM will have a ViewFrame object to display itself. Below is an example of the window after several transactions.

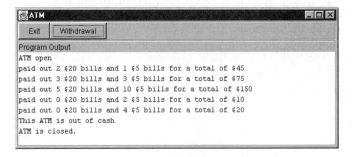

This ATM started with 10 twenties and 20 fives. When the money finally ran out it displayed the last two lines, indicating it was closing.

When the "Withdrawal" button is pressed, the machine will request the user to enter the amount as a multiple of $5 (without the dollar sign). If the user enters an amount like 34 or a negative value, the program displays a warning message using a pop-up dialog (recall that ViewFrame has a `showWarningMsg` method) and waits for the button to be pushed again.

Once a proper amount has been entered, the ATM will pay out as many $20 bills as possible, then use $5 bills for the rest. For example, if $65 is requested, the ATM will try to pay out three $20 bills and a single $5 bill. It will display the message

```
paid out 3 $20 bills and 1 $5 bill for a total of $65
```
in the output area of the window.

It is possible that the ATM will have insufficient funds to meet the request. If so, a pop-up warning message will display, saying the ATM has insufficient cash. (Again, use the `showWarningMsg` method of ViewFrame.)

Hints on Computations

If `amt` stands for the amount requested, then you can use `amt / 20` to get the maximum number of twenties you should give out. Recall that in integer division this gives the quotient.

It is possible that there may be enough money but a limited number of $20 bills. For example, if the ATM had one $20 bill and 30 $5 bills, then a $65 request would get the single $20 bill and nine $5 bills. You can handle this with the expression

```
int t;
t = Math.min(twenties, amt / 20);
```

where `twenties` is the name of the variable containing the current number of $20 bills in the ATM. `t` is now the *actual* number of $20 bills that the ATM will dispense. This avoids the use of some if-else statements.

Once you know how many $20 bills will be dispensed (`t`), you must see how many $5 bills are required to complete the withdrawal request. That is given by

```
int f;
f = (amt - t * 20) / 5;
```

Now all we have to do is see if we have that many $5 bills available. If so, we give out the money, reducing our stock of $20 and $5 bills. If not, we display "insufficient cash" in a warning window. This requires a Java if statement.

The code described above will go in the `actionPerformed` method associated with the Withdrawal button and will involve some if statements. If you wish to leave the actionPerformed method early, i.e., without executing additional statements, give the statement

```
return;
```

Notice it is not "return *expression;*" as `actionPerformed` is a procedure, not a function. For example, if a negative value was entered, you could have the statement

```
if (amt < 0)
{
    vf.showWarningMsg("Invalid amount entered.");
    return;
}
```

The return statement prevents the execution of any more statements in `actionPerformed`.

Step by Step

- Compile the project and run it. Currently, nothing happens when the button is pressed.
- The message "ATM is open" is displayed when the ATM becomes visible. At the end of the constructor after the call to setVisible you should add the statement
  ```
  vf.println("ATM is open");
  ```
- Have your action associated with the pressing of the Withdrawal button (this action is in the method actionPerformed) to initially just get the amount and display it in the output window. You may just want to

uncomment the `vf.setIOEcho(true)` statement in the constructor. Compile and run this.

- Add the data declarations for `twenties` and `fives` as discussed above. If you don't know where they should go, ask! They both should be integers. Initialize them in the constructor using t and f. Just to be certain you have the data members set up correctly, use the `vf.println()` method to print out the values of `twenties` and `fives` just before the constructor method finishes.

- Now try to get the logic correct that will dispense the bills or indicate insufficient cash on hand for the request. This requires some thought and is not easy. Don't expect to just dash something off and have it work the first time.

When you give out the money don't forget to decrease the values of `twenties` and `fives`. You will also have to figure out how to know when there is no money at all and the ATM should be closed.

When you and your partner complete the project, be sure your names are in a comment in the `ATM.java` file. Turn in a printout.

Post-Laboratory Exercises and Readings

Exercises

The file `XXXXXXXX.java` can be used as a template for classes like ATM. For simplicity, it contains a main method so you can create a single file program. Let's create a "cloning" class. It will have a window with a button that when pressed will create another version of itself. Here are the steps:

- Close any projects that might be open.
- In the IDE's editing window, open XXXXXXXX.java.
- With your cursor at the very beginning of the file, select `Edit>Replace`. When the box pops up, replace all occurrences of XXXXXXXX (eight upper-case Xs) with `CLONE`.
- Perform a "Save As" and name it `CLONE.java`.
- Remove the comment about the replacement and put in your name as the programmer.
- In the constructor use "Clone Machine" for the ViewFrame's title.
- In the constructor use "Clone Me!" for the label that will be on the button.

We won't have any data members except the ViewFrame object `vf`, so there is no more to do except fill in the `actionPerformed` method.

- In the `actionPerformed` method add the single line

  ```
  new CLONE();
  ```

Save the file, compile it, and run it. When the window appears, move it from the upper-left corner to another location on the screen. Then press the "Clone Me!" button.

You can press any of the clone's buttons and a new clone will be made. Unfortunately all clones will initially appear at the upper-left corner and may hide each other. We will fix that problem with the modification below.

Killing one window kills them all.

Modification

We want to make the vf window appear at a random location on the screen. The statement

```
vf.setLocation(50,10);
```

will locate the upper-left corner of the ViewFrame object vf 50 pixels from the left border and 10 pixels from the top border of the screen. Unfortunately, if we used this all windows would appear at this spot!

To get a random location we will select a random integer from 0 to 99 for the first coordinate of the setLocation method. The expression

```
(int)(Math.random() * 100)
```

will give us the desired random integer. We will select a random value from 0 to 49 for the second coordinate. This will be done by a similar expression using 50 instead of 100. This will work because Math.random() gives a random number from 0.0 up to but less than 1.0.

In the constructor just before the vf.setVisible(true); statement, add the lines

```
vf.setLocation((int)(Math.random() * 100), // horizontal offset
               (int)(Math.random() * 50)); // vertical offset
```

Recompile and run the program again. Do the cloned windows appear at differing locations?

Extension

This example has no data members except for the ViewFrame vf. Think about an identifying name associated with each CLONE object. If the main method created several CLONE objects, each object would create clones with their own names. The main method might look like

```
public static void main(String[] args)
{
    new CLONE("Fred");
    new CLONE("Sarah");
    new CLONE("Joe");
}
```

This would require that the constructor have a single String parameter, as in

```
public CLONE(String n) // n is the name
{
    ...
}
```

Remembering the name requires another data member like

```
String name;
```

Add its declaration to the class, and in the constructor have

```
name = n;
```

Of course during cloning you would use an instruction like

```
new CLONE(name);
```

Make the indicated changes. Recompile and run the program. Close the project.

4

Repeating Means Looping

This laboratory will focus on the ability to repeat Java statements. For example, it is not hard to have a message display twice—simply type the output statement twice. But it is tedious to display it 2,000 times by writing the output statement 2,000 times. Fortunately Java provides "looping" statements of two types—`while` statements and `for` statements—to make the task nearly trivial.

We will examine some examples of these statements in the pre-laboratory reading.

Pre-Laboratory Reading

Simple Console Output— A Note

Most computer operating systems support some type of console window (it might be called a "terminal window") where textual commands can be typed directly to the system without using a graphical interface. On Windows systems the Command Prompt window, formerly called the MS-DOS Prompt window, serves this purpose (`Start>Programs>Command Prompt`).

It is always possible to send output to the console screen when an application is running in a Command Prompt window or to send it to your IDE's output window when running within the IDE with the statement

```
System.out.println( ... );
```

where a `String` must go in the parentheses. This is a simple and primitive alternative to the graphics output you might use with a ViewFrame object `vf`:

```
vf.println( ... );
```

`System.out` is a special output stream object associated with the console screen. Some of the examples use `System.out` rather than create a ViewFrame object. This is done to reduce the size of the examples.

Syntax of a while Loop

A `while` loop has the following syntax:

```
while ( boolean condition )
{
    statements
}
```

Semantics of a while Loop

When the execution of a program reaches the beginning of a while loop, the boolean condition is checked. If it is true, the statements in the braces are executed, one after the other. When the last statement inside the braces is executed, the boolean condition is checked again. If it is true, the statements are re-executed, then the condition is checked again, and so on. If the boolean condition is ever false when checked, the statements inside the braces are skipped and we execute whatever comes after the while statement.

Normally, the statements in the while loop will modify something so that the boolean condition is eventually false.

Example 1

```
int count = 1;
while (count < 5)
{
    System.out.println("count is " + count);
    count = count + 1;
}
```

The output of the statements:

```
count is 1
count is 2
count is 3
count is 4
```

When count becomes 5 the boolean condition fails and we skip the statements in the loop.

A Common Error

The most common error is accidentally omitting the line that causes a change to the boolean condition. For example, if the line

```
count = count + 1;
```

were omitted, then the boolean condition would never be false as count would never change. These statements would print the same line forever!

Another Example

The previous example performed a task a predetermined number of times (four). Often we want to repeat a task until something happens. We won't know in advance how many times to perform the task.

Consider playing a game many times. We want to ask the user when to quit or continue. This requires that we get an answer. Of course any answer is usually a *string*, i.e., some sequence of characters. In Java, a String class is used to hold a block of characters. The ViewFrame class has a readString method, which returns the characters entered by the user at the keyboard. We use it in the next example to determine when to stop or continue.

Example 2

```
// assume we have a ViewFrame object vf
String answer;
answer = vf.readString("Do you wish to play the game?(y/n)");
answer = answer.trim(); // see digression below
while (answer.charAt(0) == 'y' ||
        answer.charAt(0) == 'Y')
{
    // do the task or game here


    answer = vf.readString("Do you wish to play again?(y/n)");
    answer = answer.trim();
}
```

Notice that prior to the start of the while loop we read the first response. Then notice that at the end of the while loop we request another response. Unless we request another response, answer will always have the same value!

Digression and comment on the use of String operations:
The String class has many useful methods:
- trim() removes any leading and trailing white space, such as blank spaces or tabs.
- charAt(p) gives the character at position p in the string. Zero is the first position.

Programs that Loop a Fixed Number of Times

The following program will print the square roots of the numbers from 1 to 36, one per line. This is a *counted* while loop. We used the file name Roots.java.

Example 3

```
// Roots.java
public class Roots
{
    public static void main(String[] args)
    {
        int count = 1;
        while (count <= 36)
        {
```

```
            System.out.println("Square root of " + count +
                    " is " + Math.sqrt(count));
            count = count + 1;
        }
    }
}
```

Practice Questions

1. How would you modify the program to display the square roots of only the *odd* numbers from 1 to 36? Indicate the changes here.

2. How would you modify the original program to display the *squares* of the numbers from 1 to 45, one per line? Indicate the changes here.

3. How would you modify the program to use a ViewFrame object for output?

4. How would you modify the program to let the user tell you what to replace 36 with?

An Alternative Format for Counted Loops: The for Loop

The for loop is primarily used for loops that will be done a predetermined number of times. It is a convenience only. Everything that the for loop does can be done by a while loop!

Syntax of for

```
for (initial expression; boolean condition; change-expression)
{
    statements
}
```

The `initial expression` is *optional* and typically sets the starting value of a variable that will be the counter. When the `boolean expression` is false, the loop is skipped. Otherwise, the statements are executed. After the statements in the loop body are executed, the *optional* `change-expression` is evaluated. Then the boolean condition is checked. The change-expression is typically where the counter variable is modified.

Relation to a while Loop

The syntax for the above for loop is equivalent to the following:

```
initial_expression;
while ( boolean condition )
{
    statements
```

```
            change_expression;
         }
```

It is important to keep this relationship between the for and while loops in mind.

The example in the previous section could have been modified to use a for loop as shown below.

Example 4

```
// Roots.java
// modified to use a for loop instead of a while loop
public class Roots
{
 public static void main(String[] args)
  {
   for (int count = 1; count <= 36; count = count + 1)
    {
    System.out.println("Square root of " + count +
                " is " + Math.sqrt(count));
    }
  }
}
```

We have put the three expressions in bold. The initial expression actually declares the variable count and gives it a starting value.

Loops with Repetitions Determined Only When the Program Runs

Consider the following example, where we ask the user to enter values that we will add up. The user signals that she or he is finished by entering a special value—in this case a negative number.

Example 5

```
// Sum.java
import LabPkg.*;
public class Sum
{
    public static void main(String[] args)
    {
    ViewFrame vf = new ViewFrame("Sum Example");
    vf.setIOEcho(true); // echo input values to output window
    vf.setVisible(true);

    int sum = 0;
    int value = vf.readInt("Enter your whole numbers using" +
                " a negative value to signal " +
                "the end of the list.");
    while (value >= 0)
     {
       sum = sum + value;  //adds current to running total
       value = vf.readInt("Next value please"); // get next number
     }
    vf.println("Total is " + sum);
    }
}
```

Notice that when the user types a negative value, the condition of the while loop becomes false and the looping terminates. Also notice how we use the variable sum to maintain a running total of the values.

For practice use your IDE to create the file Sum.java, save it, compile it, and run it several times.

nent

We have seen both the `while` and `for` loops used in the most common ways. It would be possible for Java to have only a `while` loop but the `for` loop is natural when doing something a fixed number of times.

Using the Canvas Class and the Graphics Class (optional)[1]

Among the many graphics components provided by Java, the `Canvas` class is probably the most basic. It allows the drawing or painting of various shapes and text, the setting of the foreground and background colors, and the displaying of images. Most of the work is done by methods of the `Graphics` class.

A `Graphics` object maintains all of the critical information concerning certain characteristics of visual components. It also has methods that carry out the drawing of shapes and text.

Every Java class that extends `Component` has a `Graphics` object associated with it and has a method `getGraphics()` that provides access to it.

The code below creates a `Canvas` object, adds it to an existing `ViewFrame` object so we can see it, and then draws a simple rectangle with the upper-left corner at coordinates (40,10) and a width of 100 and a height of 70. It then displays some text via the `drawString` method. The real work is done by the `Graphics` object g associated with the `Canvas` object c. This example is available for downloading with the lab if you would like to compile and run it. Try changing some positions.

```java
// DrawRectangleExample.java
import java.awt.*;
import LabPkg.*;

public class DrawRectangleExample
{
    public static void main(String[] args)
    {
        ViewFrame vf = new ViewFrame("Canvas Use Example");
        vf.setVisible(true);
        vf.setResizable(false); // we don't want any resizing of the window

        Canvas c = new Canvas();
        // set its size or the size will be 0 by 0
        c.setSize(ViewFrame.WIDTH, ViewFrame.HEIGHT / 2);
        c.setBackground(Color.yellow);
        vf.setCanvas(c); // adds or changes the ViewFrame object's Canvas

        Useful.pause(20); // wait two seconds before starting to draw
        Graphics g = c.getGraphics();
        g.drawRect(40,10,100,70);
        g.drawString("This is text.", 45,25);
    }
}
```

You will probably want to look up the documentation on `Graphics` that is part of the `java.awt` package. You will find many other methods for drawing. You may want to try some out.

The method call `Useful.pause(20);` is needed and is explained in the section on the use of `repaint` and `paint` methods.

---

1. The laboratory does not depend on the use of the Canvas class. But this useful class does provide the ability to do more interesting examples and will reappear in a few later laboratories.

Using a Canvas Object with a ViewFrame

In the previous example we did the following steps:

- created a `ViewFrame` object
- created a `Canvas` object
- called the `setCanvas` method to make our canvas appear in the `ViewFrame`

It is possible to create a Canvas object first and *automatically* make it a part of the ViewFrame object `vf` when it is created. Then the `setCanvas` method is used only to change the canvas in the ViewFrame object. The code is shown below. Notice that the creation of the ViewFrame uses a second parameter to the constructor: `c`.

```java
// DrawRectangleExampleAlt.java
import java.awt.*;
import LabPkg.*;

public class DrawRectangleExampleAlt
{
    public static void main(String[] args)
    {
        Canvas c = new Canvas();
        // set its size or the size will be 0 by 0
        c.setSize(ViewFrame.WIDTH, ViewFrame.HEIGHT / 2);
        c.setBackground(Color.yellow);

        ViewFrame vf = new ViewFrame("Canvas Use Example", c);
        vf.setVisible(true);
        vf.setResizable(false); // we don't want any resizing of the window

        Useful.pause(20); // wait two seconds before staring to draw
        Graphics g = c.getGraphics();
        g.drawRect(40,10,100,70);
        g.drawString("This is text.", 45,25);
    }
}
```

It is up to you which method you prefer to use when using a Canvas object with a ViewFrame object.

repaint() and paint()—Some Graphical Technicalities

Whenever a window appears on the screen or a window is resized, there is an automatic call to the window's `repaint` method. This method ultimately causes the `paint` method to be called after doing some other essential work (that is not important in this discussion). Every Java class that extends Component has repaint and paint methods. The repaint method has no parameters. The paint method has the current Graphics object for the visual component as a parameter.

It is the default action of the `paint` method that forced us to not allow resizing of the Canvas c in the previous example. If a rectangle were drawn and the window resized, the `repaint` method would be called. This would call the `paint` method. All it would do is redraw the canvas using the background color; no foreground would be drawn. Essentially everything on the canvas would appear to be erased.

This is also why we used the statement

`Useful.pause(20);`

to wait two seconds before starting the drawing. The `vf.setVisible(true)` call starts the process of making the window appear on the screen. *The program continues to run while this is happening.* The display takes long enough that the instructions to draw on the canvas would have finished without our pause. The last thing that happens when a window appears is a call to repaint() and hence to paint(), which would erase the canvas' drawings by painting a blank background over them. By pausing, we stop the program from continuing and allow the initial paint method call to complete before we draw our rectangle. By not allowing resizing, we prevent the repaint method (and hence the paint method) from ever being called.[2]

Extending Canvas

You can avoid some of the problems due to calls to repaint() by creating a special canvas and rewriting the paint method. An example is shown below. The specialized Canvas class is after the public class. It is not very versatile, but it illustrates the point.

```java
// DrawRectangleExampleAlt2.java
import java.awt.*;
import LabPkg.*;

public class DrawRectangleExampleAlt2
{
    public static void main(String[] args)
    {
        Canvas c = new SpecialCanvas();
        // set its size or the size will be 0 by 0
        c.setSize(ViewFrame.WIDTH, ViewFrame.HEIGHT / 2);
        c.setBackground(Color.yellow);

        ViewFrame vf = new ViewFrame("Canvas Use Example", c);
        vf.setVisible(true);
    }
}

class SpecialCanvas extends Canvas
{

    public void paint(Graphics g)
    {
        g.drawRect(40,10,100,70);
        g.drawString("This is text.", 45,25);
    }
}
```

Review Questions

1. True or False:

   a. A while loop statement is not needed in Java, provided that the for loop statement is available.

   b. A for loop statement is not needed in Java, provided that the while loop statement is available.

   c. In a while loop, the boolean condition is checked after each statement in the body of the loop is executed.

   d. In a for loop like the one below, the value of the variable i is restricted to this for loop and its statements; i.e., the value is not accessible before or after the for loop.

   ```java
   for (int i = 1; i < 99; i = i + 1)
   {
   ```

---

2. Actually, this is not quite true. If another window were placed on top and then removed, repaint would be called.

```
    . . .
  }
```

    e. Use a while loop to display the even numbers from 2 to 200, one per line, on the screen, using `System.out.println`.

2. Rewrite the following while loop as a for loop:

```
int count = 5;
while (count > 0)
{
  System.out.println("" + count);
  count = count - 1;
}
```

3. Rewrite the for loop below using a while loop statement:

```
int sum = 0;
for (int i = 1; i < 99; i = i + 1)
{
  sum = sum + i;
}
```

The Laboratory

Objectives

- To enable you to gain experience with while loops and for loops in simple situations.
- To combine drawing on a Canvas object with looping to create interesting patterns.

A Guide to the Laboratory

You will complete four tasks, each requiring you write a program from scratch using a single file. You will turn in printouts of the following files:

- `DownWhile.java`
  Uses a while loop to display the values 25, 24, ... , 1
- `DownFor.java`
  Uses a for loop to display the values 25, 24, ... , 1
- `Factors.java`
  Requests a positive integer and displays its positive factors
- `Perfect.java`
  Requests a positive integer and determines if it is "perfect" or not

All files use a ViewFrame object for input and output. The first two programs start up, do work, and show results. The last two start up, get a positive integer value, do work, and display the results.

Preliminaries

As usual, copy any files used in this lab from your diskette to your `lab_files` folder.

Task 1: A Simple Down Counter—A while Loop Version

Create a Java program file `DownWhile.java`. The program must use a while loop to display the numbers from 25 to 1 in descending order, one value per line. Output might look like

```
25
24
23
.
.
.
2
1
```

As usual, use a ViewFrame for displaying the output. (No canvas will be used.)

After testing the program, print out a copy to turn in. Be sure your name is in a comment. If you had a partner, include both names.

Task 2: A for Loop Version

Create a Java source file `DownFor.java`. The program must use a `for` loop to display the numbers from 25 to 1 in descending order, one value per line. The output will be the same as in the while loop version.

After testing the program, print out a copy to turn in. Be sure your name is in a comment. If you had a partner, include both names.

Task 3: Finding Positive Factors

You are to write a program in a file called `Factors.java` that will ask the user to enter a positive integer. The program will then display all the positive factors of that integer. For example, if the user entered 12, then the program would display

```
1
2
3
4
6
12
```

If the user entered 13, then the program would display

```
1
13
```

If the user does not enter a positive integer, display the message "Invalid input" and nothing else.

Recall that x is a positive factor of y if

- `x >= 1` and
- `y % x == 0`, i.e., there is no remainder when the division is done.

When we write the program, if we start the variable x (representing the possible factors) at the value of 1 and work upwards to the value y entered by the user, then for each value of x we can check `y % x == 0` to see if that value of x is a positive factor of y. Of course if the condition is true, we display the value of x. *Warning:* This uses both a while and an if statement.

After testing the program, print out a copy to turn in. Be sure your name is in a comment. If you had a partner, include both names.

Task 4: Perfect Numbers

Create a program in a file `Perfect.java` that will have a button labelled "Check for Perfect." When the button is pressed, the user will be prompted to enter a positive integer. One of the two messages "The number is perfect" or "The number is imperfect" will then be displayed.

A positive integer is *perfect* if it equals the sum of all its proper positive factors. A factor of a number is proper if it does not equal the number. For example, the first perfect number is 6, which equals $1 + 2 + 3$.

Start the process with the following steps to save most of the typing required to create a file with a ViewFrame with a button.

1. Open the file XXXXXXXX.java in the IDE and replace all occurrences of XXXXXXXX with Perfect.

2. Do a "Save As" using the name Perfect.java.

3. Be sure your name is in the comment at the beginning of the file.

4. Make the title of the ViewFrame window "Perfect Tester," and make the button have the label "Check for Perfect."

5. Save and compile the file. It has its own simple main method.

6. Now add the code to the actionPerformed method that

   ▪ gets a positive integer from the user

   ▪ checks to see if it is perfect or not

   ▪ displays the appropriate message

Hint: If you wish to add numbers that you see one at a time, use a variable, say sum, that starts at 0.

```
int sum = 0;
```

Then if you encounter a value, say x, that you wish to add to your total, it can be done with the statement

```
sum = sum + x;
```

Be sure your name is in a comment, plus the name of your lab partner, if you have one.

Post-Laboratory Exercises

Working with Numbers

Exercise 1

A whole number is prime if it is 2 or larger and its only possible positive factors are 1 and itself. Examples of primes are 2, 3, 5, 7, 11, 13, 17, 19, 23, 29, 31, and 37.

If N is given a positive integer value larger than 1, write code that will use a loop to determine if N is a prime number or not. Your code should then display an appropriate message.

Exercise 2

A useful fact about sequences of integers is that for any given positive integer N, we have the formula

```
1 + 2 + ... + N = N * (N + 1) / 2
```

Write a program that asks a user to enter a number N, computes the left and right sides of the formula separately, and displays each result. Reread the hint at the end of task 4 of the laboratory as you think about how to determine the left-hand sum.

Exercise 3

A computerized cash register or point-of-sale terminal in a retail store executes the following algorithm for each customer. (Of course, in the real world "ask for the price of the next item" would likely be replaced by a scanning of the item's product code.)

```
set customer's subtotal to 0
ask if there is an item
while (there are more items)
{
   ask for the price of the next item
   add price to customer's subtotal
   ask if there is another item
}
calculate tax on subtotal
display subtotal, tax, and grand total
```

Write a complete program that implements this algorithm assuming a sales tax of 4.5%.

Drawing Concentric Rectangles

Exercise 4

You are to modify the `DrawRectangleExample.java` file so that it draws concentric rectangles approximately like the picture below.

(10,10)

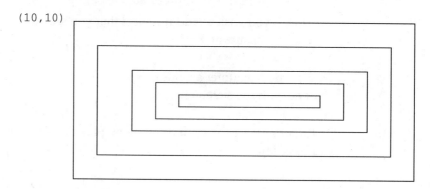

The first rectangle is to be drawn with the upper-left corner at (10,10), a width equal to ViewFrame.WIDTH - 20, and a height equal to ViewFrame.HEIGHT / 2 - 20. Each successive rectangle is inset 10 pixels on each side. Thus each new rectangle is 20 pixels narrower and 20 pixels shorter than the prior one.

Stop drawing rectangles when either the current length or the current width is less than 10 pixels. Be sure to put your name in a comment. Print out a copy to turn in.

Exercise 5

The method `drawOval` of the `Graphics` class draws an oval within an invisible rectangle. If the rectangle is a square it draws a circle.

Modify the previous exercise to draw concentric ovals instead of rectangles.

Exercise 6

Revise your program in exercise 4 that draws concentric rectangles so that the drawing is done in the `paint` method of a class that extends the `Canvas` class. (This is the idea presented in the third example of drawing rectangles on a canvas.) Then instead of using `ViewFrame.WIDTH - 20` and `ViewFrame.HEIGHT / 2 - 20` for the initial dimensions, get the actual dimensions of the canvas with

```
Dimension d = getSize(); // within the paint method
```
Then start the first rectangle with the width `d.width - 20`. The height will be `d.height - 20`.

Now you can allow resizing and the rectangles will adjust their shape while retaining their concentric pattern.

A Fun Example—The Random Walk

The file `RandomWalk.java` contains a program that
- draws a square in the middle of a canvas
- starting at the center of the square, draws a short line in one of the four directions (up, down, right, and left) at random
- repeats the previous step, starting from the other end of the newly drawn line, until it reaches the boundary indicated by the square

Compile it and run it.

We use a `Die` class that comes with the LabPkg package. A `Die` object is given an initial number of sides; the number must be a positive integer. In this case, the number is 4 because we want to go in one of four directions. A `Die` object can then provide a random whole number from 1 to 4. The programmer determines which values correspond to which directions.

The `Die` method `valueOf()` returns the current random value. The method `roll()` gets another random value, possibly the same value.

Exercise 7

Try to modify `RandomWalk.java` so that a line drawn has the length 20 rather than 10. This will make it more likely to reach the boundary faster.

Exercise 8

Try to modify `RandomWalk.java` so it never does a reverse; e.g., if it just moved up, it cannot move down on the next move—only left, right, or up. This should also give it a greater chance of reaching the boundary more quickly. It also requires a data member to record the previous direction moved. Initialize the data member to 0.

LABORATORY 5

String Basics and Applications

While computers were originally sold to perform high-speed arithmetic calculations, a significant number of modern applications are text-oriented. Word-processing software and spelling checkers immediately come to mind. Such software works with "strings."

In all computer languages, a "string" is a block of characters with a length (the number of characters in it) that can be determined and with individual characters that can be accessed. Typically a language provides the following additional operations:

- comparison of two strings to determine lexicographical (like in a dictionary) order or equality
- concatenation of two strings to produce a new string
- search for a specified substring
- conversion of all characters in a string from upper case to lower case or vice versa

In Java, strings are implemented as `String` objects. The purpose of this laboratory is to examine the `String` class and its methods. We will make use of the primitive character type `char` when we look at individual characters.

Pre-Laboratory Reading

Documentation

The `String` class is part of the `java.lang` package. You should find the documentation for it at the URL

`http://java.sun.com/j2se/1.3/docs/api/index.html`

If you open the file

`file:///A:/index.html`

in your browser, you can follow the documentation links to Sun Microsystems' online Java documentation.

This discussion can look at only a few of the many available methods. Others are described (briefly) in the documentation.

String Basics

In Java a String object maintains a block of characters as part of its data. The number of characters in the block is called the length of the string. A method `length()` provides the value of the length of the string, i.e., how many characters the String object holds.

Each character in the block has a position. The initial position is 0. The final position number is one less than the length of the string. The string `"Jean"` has the length 4. `'J'` is at position 0, `'e'` is at position 1, `'a'` is at position 2, and `'n'` is at position 3. Notice again that the final position, 3, is one less than the length, 4.

Recall that explicit individual characters are indicated with apostrophes (commonly called single quotes), as in `'J'`. `"J"` is not a character; it is a String literal containing one character. Be careful of this distinction when working with single characters.

String Literals

We used String literals in our earliest programs. String literals are explicit sequences of characters delimited by quotation marks (normal double quotes, not apostrophes). Examples are

```
"hello"
"This is a longer string literal."
""
"256"
```

The third example is called an *empty string*. (There is no space between the quotation marks!) It has zero characters but is still considered a valid String literal. The last example is not a number, but is a block of characters.

String literals are instances of the String class that are created by the compiler. As objects they have access to all the methods of the String class. The expression

```
"hello".toUpperCase()
```

has as its value the String object `"HELLO"`. However, we rarely use String literals in this way.

There are times when we want a quotation mark to be part of the String literal. How can we do this? We simply put a backslash symbol in front of the quote symbol. For example

```
vf.println("This is a very \"special\" time for me.");
```

will display the message

```
This is a very "special" time for me.
```

on the output portion of the ViewFrame object vf. The backslash symbol indicates that the quotation mark immediately following it is not the end of the String literal.

Warning: Be careful to use the symbol \ and not the division symbol / when you intend a backslash. On most keyboards the backslash symbol is just above the **Enter** key and below the **Backspace** key.

Declaring and Creating Strings

A variable of type String is a reference to some String object stored in the computer's memory or is a variable with the value null.[1] The following is the most common type of declaration and initialization of a String variable:

```
String  name = "John Smithson";
```

An alternative would be

```
String name = new String("John Smithson");
```

The latter explicitly creates a new String object that is a copy of the "John Smithson" String literal. Most beginning programmers will not care about this distinction.

It is always possible to declare a String variable and give it a value later—prior to its use. Either of the following forms will work:

```
String word = null;
String lastname;   // implicitly has value null
```

Just remember that such variables must be assigned values before being used in any expression.

String Operations and Methods

Concatenation

The operations that are signaled by operators such as +, *, -, <, ==, and so on are restricted in Java to just the primitive types, like int, double, and char. You cannot compare two objects with == and get the result you expect!

However, there is one exception—the plus symbol (+) can be used with String objects and means *concatenation*. The concatenation of two strings is a new string with the character block created by taking copies of the characters from the first String object and following them with copies of the characters from the second String object. For example, if we have the declarations

```
String w1 = "the";
String w2 = "re";
```

then w1 + w2 is the new String object "there".

Java also can convert primitive types to String objects in the context of concatenation. For example, suppose x is an integer variable with the value 56, then

```
"The value is " + x
```

is the String object "The value is 56". The compiler sees that one part of the + expression is a String and automatically performs concatenation. This requires that the integer value of x be converted to a String object, so that is done automatically.

---

1. null is the special value used in Java to indicate that a reference is not referring to any object.

If a method requires a String argument and is given an integer variable, the conversion to String is *not* done automatically. But when the variable is concatenated with an empty string, you get the proper result. Continuing the above example, if vf is a ViewFrame object, then

```
vf.println( "" + x );
```

will display "56" without the quotation marks. The program is not displaying the number 56, but the characters '5' and '6'. We simply think of it as showing the number!

What is the output of the following two statements?

```
vf.println( x + x + "" );
vf.println( "" + x + x );
```

This is a little tricky, but the first statement will display "112" without the quotation marks. The addition of integers is done first and then that answer is converted to a String. The second statement displays "5656" without the quotation marks. Why? Well, the order of operations for the second expression is

```
"" + x
```

and then

```
"56" + x
```

Notice that `"" + x` gives `"56"`. One operand is a String, so x's value, 56, is converted to a String and concatenation with the empty String object is performed. The second step is again conversion and concatenation.

No confusion results with other operators, like * or -, and strings.

trim

We often get a response from a user and want to ignore any leading or trailing spaces or tabs. The trim method does this for us. An example is

```
String response = vf.readString("What is your first name?");
response = response.trim();
```

The second line replaces the value of `response` with its trimmed version. If there were no spaces or tabs at the beginning or end of the string, then nothing would change.

equals

As mentioned above, we use `==` to compare only primitive values. String objects must be compared using special methods. This makes sense, as they are not simple things.

To test for the equality of two String variables, x and y, one uses the expression

```
x.equals(y)
```

which is either true or false—the method is boolean. True is returned provided all the characters of x are the same as the characters of y and their positions and case match. Of course if the above were true, then `y.equals(x)` would also be true.

If you want to compare two strings but ignore the case of individual characters, use the method `equalsIgnoreCase` provided by the String class.

compareTo

Strings are generally compared using lexicographical order, or dictionary order. This is the ordering we would use to alphabetize a list of words. However, computers distinguish between upper and lower case. In general all the upper-case characters precede any lower-case characters. Within the upper-case characters, the ordering is normal: A, then B, and so on. Similarly for the lower-case characters.

The `compareTo` method returns an integer with the following meanings:

```
x.compareTo(y) == 0      // x equals y
x.compareTo(y) < 0       // x precedes y lexicographically
x.compareTo(y) > 0       // x comes after y
```

There is a method `compareToIgnoreCase` if you want to ignore case differences.

charAt

The `charAt` method simply returns the character at the specified position.

```
x.charAt(4)
```

gives the character at position 4. Of course the position must be valid for the string or the program will crash with an `IndexOutOfBounds` exception message. (The position of a character is often called the *index* of the character.)

Characters

As we know, `char` is a primitive type. As such, it is available for comparisons such as

```
if (c >= 'a' && c <= 'z')
{
    vf.println("It is lower case alphabetic.");
}
```

where c is a variable of type `char`. Also, if two variables `c1` and `c2` are of the type `char`, then they can be compared for equality with `c1 == c2`.

There is a special class `Character` that contains a number of useful static methods relating to characters. We list some examples below, where we assume c is a variable of type `char`. (The class `Character` is in the package `java.lang`, which is automatically available to all Java programs.)

- `Character.isDigit(c)`—returns true if c is one of the characters '0' or '1' or ... '9'
- `Character.isLetter(c)`—returns true if c is a letter of the alphabet
- `Character.isLowerCase(c)`—returns true only if c is a lower-case character
- `Character.isUpperCase(c)`—returns true only if c is an upper-case character
- `Character.isWhitespace(c)`—returns true only if c is a white space character like a space, tab, or newline
- `Character.toUpperCase(c)`—returns the upper-case version of c if c is lower case, otherwise it returns c
- `Character.toLowerCase(c)`—returns the lower-case version of c if c is an upper-case character, otherwise it returns c

In addition, an instance of the class `Character` can be used when an object is required but what you have is a character. For example,

```
Character charObject = new Character('a');
```

allows us to wrap the primitive character `'a'` into an object. Then the expression

```
charObject.charValue()
```

will be the character `'a'`. Sometimes Character is called a *wrapper class*, as it allows us to convert a primitive value into an object.

Some Example Programs

All of these examples are available for downloading. You may wish to compile and run each as you read along.

Example 1

In this example we read in a string and display its characters one at a time in reverse order. As usual we use a ViewFrame object for input and output.

```java
// ReverseStringV1.java
// we read in a string and display its characters one per line in
// reverse order, from last character to first character
import LabPkg.*;

public class ReverseStringV1
{
    public static void main(String[] args)
    {
        ViewFrame vf = new ViewFrame("ReverseStringV1");
        vf.setVisible(true);
        vf.setIOEcho(true);

        String s = vf.readString("Enter some characters");
        int len = s.length();
        vf.println("The characters in reverse are:");
        for (int i = len - 1; i >= 0 ; i = i - 1)
        {
            vf.println("" + s.charAt(i));
        }
    }
}
```

Notice that we used a for loop that started with the last position (which was one less than the length) and decreased toward 0, with 0 being the final position.

The output after entering the string `"last is first"` is shown below.

Example 2

We can use some of the functions of the Character class to display only the alphabetic characters in a string. Notice the minor change to the code—we simply enclose the `vf.println(""+s.charAt(i))` statement in an if statement.

```java
// ReverseStringV2.java
import LabPkg.*;
```

```
public class ReverseStringV2
{
    public static void main(String[] args)
    {
        ViewFrame vf = new ViewFrame("ReverseStringV2");
        vf.setVisible(true);
        vf.setIOEcho(true);
        String s = vf.readString("Enter some characters");
        int len = s.length();
        vf.println("The alphabetic characters in reverse are:");
        for (int i = len - 1; i >= 0 ; i = i - 1)
        {
            if (Character.isLetter(s.charAt(i)))
            {
                vf.println("" + s.charAt(i));
            }
        }
    }
}
```

Example 3

In this example we create a *new* string that is the reverse of the string entered by a user. The key is successive concatenation of single characters—we build the new string one character at a time! Try to trace the steps by hand with a simple string like `"abc"`, looking at the new value of r each time through the loop.

```
// ReverseStringV3.java
// we create a new string that is the reverse of a
// user-provided string

import LabPkg.*;

public class ReverseStringV3
{
    public static void main(String[] args)
    {
        ViewFrame vf = new ViewFrame("ReverseStringV3");
        vf.setVisible(true);
        vf.setIOEcho(true);

        String s = vf.readString(
            "Enter any characters and press the Enter key");
        String r = "";   // start r as the empty string
        int len = s.length();
        for(int i = 0; i <= len - 1; i = i + 1)
        {
            r = s.charAt(i) + r;   // notice the order
        }
        vf.println(r);
    }
}
```

It is possible to do this by means of a for loop that goes from the last position in s to the first position in s; the assignment and concatenation step would change to `r = r + s.charAt(i);`. Output is shown below for the entered string `"last is first"`:

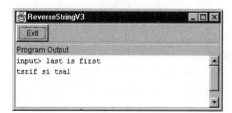

Example 4

In this example we use a special class called `StringTokenizer` to break a string into pieces and print each piece on a separate line. The pieces are called "tokens" and they are determined by "separator characters." The common separator characters are the white space characters (space, tab, and newline). A token is defined to be the biggest possible block of nonseparator characters; i.e., if another character were included at either end it would be a separator character.

You can use the StringTokenizer constructor to specify which characters are separators or you can just use the default white space characters. In the example below we use the default separators.

```
// StringTokens.java
// Illustrates the use of a StringTokenizer object

import LabPkg.*;
import java.util.*;

public class StringTokens
{
    public static void main(String[] args)
    {
        ViewFrame vf = new ViewFrame("StringTokens Example");
        vf.setVisible(true);
        vf.setIOEcho(true);

        String s = vf.readString("Enter a sentence.");
        StringTokenizer st = new StringTokenizer(s);
        // st has operations to see each token one at a time
        while (st.hasMoreTokens())
        {
            vf.println(st.nextToken());
        }
    }
}
```

The output below is what is shown when the string `"Hello! Are you ready?"` is entered.

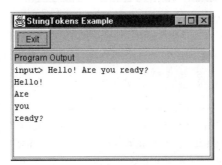

Notice that the punctuation characters `'!'` and `'?'` are not separators and so are part of the tokens. The change shown below to the declaration and initialization of `st` would use white space and some common punctuation characters as separators. The character `'\t'` is the tab character and `'\n'` is the newline character. A space character is first. Notice that we simply have a second parameter to the constructor that is a string containing all the separators.

```
StringTokenizer st = new StringTokenizer(s , " \t\n.,;:!?'\"");
```

Why are we interested in this example? If we were to write a spelling checker, we would need to examine our document as a string and break it into words. The tokens would be the words we would need. StringTokenizer is a tool class—it exists to perform the task of breaking a given string into pieces.

Because it is a tool class, it is in the package `java.util`. (Notice `import java.util.*;` in the program.)

As soon as we learn about efficient ways to create a dictionary and to look up words we can write a spelling checker. That is still several labs away.

Review Questions

1. How does one write the character that is the last letter of the alphabet in upper-case form in Java?

2. How do we set off a literal string in Java, i.e., what symbol is used?

3. Consider the declaration/definition

   ```
   String s = "THREE";
   ```

   a. What is the value of `s.length()`?

   b. What is the last position number in the string?

   c. What is the first position number in the string?

   d. What character is at position 2?

   e. What is the value of `s.charAt(1)`?

4. What symbol is used to concatenate two strings together?

5. What is the value of

   a. `5 + 5 + "5"`

   b. `"5" + 5 + 5`

   c. `"5" + (5 + 5)`

The Laboratory

Objectives

- To create programs that examine `String` objects.
- To make use of methods from the `String` class.
- To correctly use single characters as well as the method `Character.isLetter`.

A Guide to the Laboratory

You will complete three programs from scratch. Each is based on examples in the pre-laboratory reading. All make use of the method `readString("...")` of the ViewFrame class for reading in a string.

Turn in copies of the following files:

- `Vowels.java`
- `AlphaOnly.java`
- `Pal.java`

Be sure your name is in a comment at the beginning of each file.

Task 1: Counting Vowels

The vowels are the five characters `'a'`, `'e'`, `'i'`, `'o'`, and `'u'`.

Write a program in a file called `Vowels.java` that uses a ViewFrame and asks the user to enter a string. The program will then examine the characters in the string and display the number of times an `'a'` appears, the number of times an `'e'` appears, and so on, counting vowels only. It should then print out the information in a neat form.

To avoid distinctions between upper and lower case, convert the input string to lower case before you start counting.

Sample output is shown below:

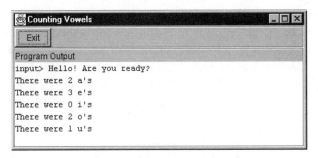

After it is working, print out a copy with your name(s) on it and turn it in.

Task 2: AlphaOnly

Write a program in a file called `AlphaOnly.java` that will read in a string and create a new string that is just the alphabetic characters in the original string. Display this new string on the output of your ViewFrame object. For example, if the input string were `"Hello! Are you ready?"` then the created string would be `"HelloAreyouready"`.

Be sure you actually create a new string and *don't* simply print individual characters to the screen using `vf.print("" + ...)`, where `vf` is a ViewFrame object.

Please print out a copy of your program file when it is working correctly.

Task 3: Palindrome

Write a program in the file `Pal.java` that will read in a string and print a message "It's a palindrome" or "It's not a palindrome" according to whether the string is or is not a palindrome.

A string is a palindrome if, after ignoring all characters except alphabetic letters and ignoring the case of those letters, the string reads the same backwards and forwards. The classic—if trivializing—example is "A man, a plan, a canal - Panama!" Other simple examples are

```
"abcBa"
"toot"
"a    b ,,, A"
""
"A"
```

Hint: You will probably want to take the original string and convert it to upper case or lower case using one of the string methods. Then you can create a string of only alphabetic letters as you did in the previous program. Finally, create a new string that is the reverse of your alphabetic string and see if your alphabetic string equals its reverse.

When your program is working, make sure your name is in a comment and print out a copy to turn in.

Post-Laboratory Exercises

Exercise 1

Write a program to read in two strings and display them in dictionary order, one string per line.

Exercise 2: PalindromeTester

Create a Java class `PalindromeTester` that has a ViewFrame with a button labelled "Test a palindrome" that when pushed will request a string and display a message indicating whether or not the string was a palindrome.

Use the template file `XXXXXXXX.java` to save time. Recall that you should

- open `XXXXXXXX.java` in the IDE's editor
- replace all occurrences of `XXXXXXXX` (eight Xs) with `PalindromeTester`
- do a "Save As" using the name `PalindromeTester.java`
- check and modify the titles for the window and the button
- fill in the `actionPerformed` method (you can reuse much of the code from the program in task 3)

The main method is part of the file and creates a `PalindromeTester` object.

Exercise 3

Write a program that will read in a string, extract the individual words using a `StringTokenizer`, and display a count of how many words are equal to `"the"` when case is ignored. Call your file `TheCount.java`.

Exercise 4

Write a program called `CaesarCipher.java` that will read in a string and produce a coded version where each alphabetic character is replaced by the letter that comes after it in the alphabet, with the `'z'` being replaced by the `'a'`. Convert the entire string to upper case before encoding. Hence the string

`"Quiz secrets are ok"`

becomes

`"RVJA TFDSFUT BSF PL"`

Exercise 5

Write two classes: `Encoder` and `Decoder`. An Encoder object has a ViewFrame with a button on it that says "Encode a string." When the button is pressed the user is prompted for a string and the Caesar cipher algorithm of exercise 4 is used to create and then display the encoded version of the string. The Decoder object simply reverses what the Encoder object does—it takes an encoded string and produces the decoded version.

Write a main class called `CoderTester` that will simply create an Encoder and a Decoder object. Put all three files in a project.

Exercise 6

Using the template file `XXXXXXXX.java`, create a class `Coder` that will have a ViewFrame object containing two buttons. One button will be labeled "Encode a String," while the other will be labeled "Decode a String." Make sure that both buttons are added as `GeneralButton` objects. In the `actionPerformed` method, you will need the following lines:

```
String cmd = e.getActionCommand(); // get the button's label
if (cmd.equals("Encode a String")
{
    ... // code for encoding
}
else
```

```
{
    ... // code for decoding
}
```

The main method simply creates a single `Coder` object.

Exercise 7

Write a program that will read in a string, eliminate all substrings that start with `'<'` and end with `'>'`, and display the resulting string. If the string were the one below with the HTML font command,

```
" Hello <font color=red>Joe</font>."
```

the cleaned up version would be

```
" Hello Joe."
```

Call the file `StripHTML.java`.

Comment

All of our programs use fairly short strings (one-liners), but later we shall see how to read the contents of a text file. This will allow us to apply these principles in a more practical way. For example, most material that would need to be encoded would be in a file or an email message. Similarly, if we were to write a spelling checker we would need to be able to read the current document file containing the term paper or letter.

6

Zip Codes and
Postal Bar Codes

The main purpose of this laboratory is to gain some practice writing methods. These methods are in the context of a class that allows the scanning of a postal bar code to detect a zip code and the generation and display of a postal bar code given a zip code. The preliminary reading and questions are designed to provide you some background on the problem.

Pre-Laboratory Reading

Introduction to Postal Bar Codes	Bar codes are graphical patterns that represent numbers. They are read by scanners. On packages like cereal boxes, the codes are composed of thick and thin bars and are part of the Universal Product Code system. In this lab we will study programs that process postal bar codes. Postal bar codes use bars that are either full or half height. Each digit requires a five-bar pattern. We will display the codes graphically, but internally we will use the characters ǀ for a full-height bar and ꞉ for a half-height bar. For example, the digit 7 is

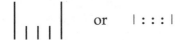

We will show both the graphical form (although with more spacing than normal) and the form we will use internally.

The Encoding	Each digit, 0 through 9, has a code. The table below shows the digit and String pairs.

Digit	String
1	"꞉꞉꞉ǀǀ"
2	"꞉꞉ǀ꞉ǀ"
3	"꞉꞉ǀǀ꞉"
4	"꞉ǀ꞉꞉ǀ"
5	"꞉ǀ꞉ǀ꞉"
6	"꞉ǀǀ꞉꞉"
7	"ǀ꞉꞉꞉ǀ"
8	"ǀ꞉꞉ǀ꞉"
9	"ǀ꞉ǀ꞉꞉"
0	"ǀǀ꞉꞉꞉"

The Rule	Every five-digit zip code, when represented using a postal bar code, has a single full-height bar at the beginning and another at the end, enclosing the patterns for the five digits plus the "check digit." Thus the code

- begins with a full-height bar,
- is followed by the codes for each of the five digits in the zip code,
- which is followed by the code for the check digit (described below),
- which is followed by a full-height bar.

The pattern goes from left to right.

The Check Digit	The check digit is calculated by adding up the digits of the five-digit zip code and seeing what would have to be added to the sum to get a multiple of 10. For example, the check digit for the zip code 51220 would be 0 (as 5 + 1 + 2 + 2 + 0 = 10), while the check digit for 82125 would be 2 (as 8 + 2 + 1 + 2 + 5 = 18).

Quick Self-Test

Give the check digit for each of the following zip codes:

- 23173
- 10064
- 00999
- 67023

The answers are 4, 9, 3, and 2, respectively.

A Basic Problem— Finding the Individual Digits of a Whole Number

When creating a postal bar code for a particular zip code, you must be able to look at each digit in the zip code individually so (1) the digits can be added to determine the check digit and (2) each digit can be replaced by its String code from the table above. The solution is to use the / and % operations. There are several possible approaches, but here are some hints.

Given the number `56734`, we can get the right-most, or "tens," digit using `56734 % 10`. We can get the left-most digit using `56734 / 10000`.

How would you get the second digit from the right (the 3 in our example)? There are two solutions:

- `(56734 % 100) / 10`
- `(56734 / 10) % 10`

Your Tasks

Write out your answers to these three questions PRIOR TO THE LABORA-TORY:

1. Consider x to be a five-digit integer. (Note that 2 is viewed as 00002 in this case.) Write Java statements that assign the five digits to D1, D2, D3, D4, and D5, where D1 is the right-most digit, D2 is the second from the right, and so on. We assume that D1 through D5 are declared to be of type int. You will use this information in the lab.

2. Suppose you have the five single digits D1 through D5 as described above, but don't have the original value of x. What Java statement would assign to x the value used to create the D1–D5 values?

3. Supposing that you have the five single digits D1 through D5 as described above, how would you compute the check digit's value?

Substrings

Task 5 of the laboratory will require that you take a string that is a bar code and select particular substrings so you can find the digits of the zip code. For example, if b is the string holding the bar code, then

`b.substring(1,6)`

is the block of characters in b from position 1 to position 5. Notice that we said 5, not 6! The second parameter in the substring method is the position immediately after the last position that is part of the substring. The first parameter is just the first position for the substring.

Review Questions

1. What character is first and last in the postal bar code pattern?
2. What is the check digit for 22334?
3. If the zip code is scanned as 00721 and the check digit is scanned as 0, is the pattern likely to be correct or not? Why?

4. Given a three-digit value N, what arithmetic expression in Java will give
    a. the right-most digit?
    b. the left-most digit?
    c. the middle digit?
5. If N is an integer, 23 for example, and you want to print it as a three-digit number like 023, how can you create the string "023" from the number 23? Give the answer in terms of N. (Does your solution work if the integer is 5, when the desired result is "005"?)
6. Give the postal bar code for the zip code 10012.

The Laboratory

Objectives

- To be able to write simple methods.
- To recognize that the use of methods can save effort and make code easier to understand.
- To gain practice in the proper development and testing of your code.
- To read and modify a larger program.
- To complete and use methods involving integers and strings.

A Guide to the Laboratory

You will need to download the two files used in the laboratory from the Web page for this lab. The files are

- BarCodeCanvas.java, a class used to graphically display a postal bar code along with some text.
- BarCodeZipCodeConverter.java, a class used to "scan" bar codes and produce the zip code or to produce the bar code given a zip code. It contains a simple main method that creates an instance of the class.

You will be creating a project that will contain these two files. You will not change the BarCodeCanvas.java file, but the other file has five methods that are incomplete.

Tasks 1 through 3 require that you complete methods and then test them. They can be tested independently of the methods of tasks 4 and 5.

After all the methods are completed and the program is tested, you are to print out a copy of BarCodeZipCodeConverter.java to turn in.

A Guide to the Program Structure

The main class is BarCodeZipCodeConverter which has a ViewFrame with two additional buttons—one for getting the zip code from a bar code string and the other for getting the bar code string from a zip code. A special type of Canvas was created that can display a simple text message and a graphical version of the bar code string. It is called BarCodeCanvas. There are three inner classes in the BarCodeZipCodeConverter class:

- Scanner—a class to obtain a bar code string from the user
- Bar2ZipAction—an action button that, when pressed, causes the scanner to obtain a bar code string, decodes that string, and produces the zip code

- Zip2BarAction—an action button that, when pressed, obtains a zip code from the user and displays the corresponding postal bar code

These are inner classes so they can have access to the ViewFrame and its BarCodeCanvas.

The screen below shows the application after it converted the zip code 23173 to a postal bar code. The code actually produced the string

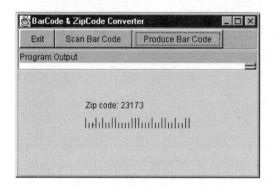

"|::|:|::||::::|||::|::||::|::||" and then the BarCodeCanvas object correctly displayed it graphically.

If the "Scan Bar Code" button were pressed, the user could enter a string like "|::|:|::||::::|||::|::||::|::||" and the program would determine that the zip code was 23173 and the check digit was (correctly) 4. The program would then display the zip code and also the bar code on the canvas. In a real-world program, the scanner object would access an optical scanning device instead of asking the user to enter a string of '|' and ':' characters.

Looking at the Program Code

If you haven't done so, create a project called BarCodeZipCode and add the two files to the project. You may want to compile both of them. They should compile although the answers will not be correct when the program runs.

Print out a copy of BarCodeZipCodeConverter.java now for reading and marking up.

The Two Key Methods

The two `actionPerformed` methods associated with the two action button classes are where the main logic is to be found. The code for scanning a bar code and producing the zip code is shown first.

```
public void actionPerformed(ActionEvent e)
{
    vf.println("Scan button pressed"); // debugging
    c.clearMessage();
    c.clearCode();
    scanner.scan();
    String code;
    code = scanner.getBarCodeString();
    int zip = convertBarCodeToZipCode(code);
    c.setMessage("Zip code: " + zipCodeString(zip));
    c.setCode(code);
}
```

The first line was just for debugging and could be omitted. The variable `c` refers to a BarCodeCanvas object that is part of the ViewFrame. The two calls to methods of `c` clear any existing messages and bar code strings. A Scanner object is used to obtain the bar code string and store it into the variable `code`. The guts of the conversion is done by a private method called `convertBarCodeToZipCode`. You will be writing this method in the lab. The last two lines call on methods of the BarCodeCanvas object `c` to display the zip code and the bar code.

The `actionPerformed` method for the other button is similar.

```
public void actionPerformed(ActionEvent e)
{
    vf.println("Convert zip code button pressed"); // debugging
    c.clearMessage();
    c.clearCode();
    int zip;
    zip = vf.readInt("Enter 5-digit zip code");
    if (!(zip >= 0 && zip <= 99999))
    {
        vf.showWarningMsg("Not valid zip code");
        return;
    }
    String code;
    code = convertZipCodeToBarCodeString(zip);
    c.setMessage("Zip code: " + zipCodeString(zip));
    c.setCode(code);
}
```

In this case we see an explicit request for the zip code followed by a check that it is legal. Again, the heart of the conversion to a postal bar code string is in the method `convertZipCodeToBarCodeString`. You will be writing this in the lab.

There is another method used in these two examples—`zipCodeString`. It writes the zip code integer as a string with any necessary leading zeroes. The zip code 123 is displayed as 00123. This is already written for you.

The Incomplete Methods	The following methods are listed in the order you need to complete them. ■ convertDigitToCode ■ getCheckDigit ■ convertZipCodeToBarCodeString ■ convertCodeToDigit ■ convertBarCodeToZipCode

---

Tasks 1–3	Complete the first three methods, carefully reading the comments, and then test the conversion of a zip code to a bar code.

Tasks 4–5 (may be done as a post-lab exercise if time is short)	When the first three methods are working, complete the final two methods and test the conversion of a bar code string to its zip code integer.

Test Data	You will need to know some zip codes and bar code strings so you can test. You should also include some illegal bar code strings and illegal zip codes in

your testing to be sure they are detected. The following are some sample zip codes and corresponding bar code strings (which include the check digit code).

Zip Code	Bar Code String
23173	"|:::|:|::||::::|||:::|::||::|::||"
00000	"|||:::||:::||:::||:::||:::||:::|"
00077	"|||:::||:::||:::|::||:::|:||::|"
99999	"||:|::|:|::|:|::|:|::|:|::|:|:|"
22903	"|:::|:|::|:||:|::||::::||::|::||"
50005	"|:|:|:||:::||:::||:::|:|:||:::|"

Hints

The first and fourth methods are just lookups in the table at the bottom of the first page of the lab. For example, in `convertDigitToCode`, if the parameter d were the digit 7 you would return the string `"|:::|"`. In the method `convertCodeToDigit`, if the string c were to equal `"|:::|"`, the method would return a 7. Both methods use an if-else-if structure.

The `getCheckDigit` method requires that you add the individual digits of the number n and determine and return the required check digit. **Be careful of the special case where the sum is a multiple of 10 and the check digit would be 0.**

The methods `convertZipCodeToBarCodeString` and `convertBarCodeToZipCode` can use the methods you have already written. This will reduce their complexity greatly.

Post-Laboratory Exercises

Exercise 1

Find a piece of bulk mail with a nine-digit zip code such as 23173-0481, and look at the postal bar code. Decode each digit. Can you figure out the coding system? If not, try to find out the system using the Internet or the library.

Exercise 2

In binary code strings of the symbols '0' and '1', a parity symbol is often added. Even parity is the most common. It works in this way: The number of '1' symbols in a string is counted. If that number is odd, the parity symbol is '1'. Otherwise, it is '0'. The goal is to have the total number of '1' symbols, with the parity symbol included, be an even number.

Write a program `Parity.java` that requests a binary string from the user and displays the string with the parity symbol added to the end.

Write another program called `CheckParity.java` that requests a binary string from the user and, assuming that a parity symbol is part of the string, displays one of the two messages "Parity Error" or "No Parity Error."

7

A Methods Toolbox

All professional software developers over the course of their careers create special functions that they reuse many times. While Java provides many useful classes, such as the Math class and StringTokenizer, it is a good idea to develop your own collection of special functions, procedures, and classes.

In this laboratory you will start the process of creating a personal collection of methods that you can use in this and other courses. In later labs we will add other methods. Today we will create a single class called Toolbox that you will keep with your project files and use as needed. Later when we add new classes we will create a package that you can import into your programs.

Pre-Laboratory Reading

Methods in General

We assume that you have already seen and used some methods, but here is a quick review of the basic ideas.

We can view a method as a collection of instructions associated with a name. The instructions make up the method body. Programming languages allow a programmer to provide special values to the method body via parameters. Some methods don't require any additional information and have no parameters.

Methods are of two types: procedures and functions. A procedure simply executes instructions and does not *return* a value. Functions *must* return a value. A procedure may be viewed as a specialized, user-defined Java statement, while a function is used where a value is desired.

Method Definitions

A method definition has the following form:

```
adjectives return_type name( parameter_list )
{
        statements
}
```

The `adjectives` part is optional, but generally consists of `public` or `private`, optionally followed by `static`. The `return_type` is the keyword `void` for a procedure and the data type of the value returned for a function. The `parameter_list` may be omitted or may be a comma-separated list of declarations of the form

```
type varable_name
```

The procedure below displays the String s some number of times determined by n.

```
public void showString(String s, int n)
{
    for (int i = 1; i <= n; i = i + 1)
    {
        System.out.println(s);
    }
}
```

Notice that the return type is void.

This method might be *called*, or activated, with the following instruction:

```
showString("dumb", 3);
```

This would display the following at the console output device:

```
dumb
dumb
dumb
```

In this example, the String s is given the value `"dumb"`, the integer n is given the value 3, and the instructions in the method are executed.

Functions are similar, but they must contain a statement of the form

```
return expression ;
```

When executed, this causes the value of the expression to be calculated and "returned." When returned, the value is put in place of the called method. In the example below,

```
double x = Math.sqrt(4.0) + 3.14;
```

the function Math.sqrt(4.0) returns a value of 2.0. So the right-hand side becomes

```
2.0 + 3.14
```
We shall see more examples below.

---

static Methods

Recall that a `static` method is one that can be called by specifying the class name instead of an object name. For example, the square root method `sqrt` of the Math class is static and is called with

```
Math.sqrt(...)
```

In some languages these are called *class methods*, as they are associated with the class definition and not an object instance.

Creating a static method requires adding the method to a class and putting the keyword `static` prior to the return type specification. The most common example is `main`.

```
public static void main(String[] args)
```

If this were in the class App, the command `java App` would be executed to run the program. It would call `App.main(...)`. It is not necessary to create an App object to call `main`.

In this laboratory we will be creating a single Java file `Toolbox.java` that will contain a Toolbox class consisting of a number of static methods. As static methods they can be called at any time without creating an instance of the Toolbox class. The only requirement is that the Toolbox class be compiled and accessible.

Calling a Toolbox Method

Suppose you had a static method in Toolbox called `printRectangle` that was a procedure and took two integer parameters. It could be called by writing

```
Toolbox.printRectangle(20, 30);
```

Notice that this statement is just the calling expression followed by a semicolon.

On the other hand, if Toolbox contained a method `isLeapYear` that took a single parameter and returned true or false according to whether the parameter was a leap year or not, then it would need to be called where a boolean value was expected.

```
if (Toolbox.isLeapYear(y))
```

The boldface expression is placed where a boolean is expected.

An Example

Consider a function that will provide a floating point value that is rounded to a specified number of decimal places. The function would look like

```
public static double roundDouble(double d, int precision)
{
    ...
}
```

where a comment would show that precision must be non-negative and at most 8. (In practice, the most common values for precision would be 0 to 2.) If a precision out of the range is passed into the function, the function will return the value of d.

The body of this function looks fairly simple, but there is a lot going on.

```
if (precision < 0 || precision > 8)
{
    return d;
}
else
{
    long p;
```

```
        p = 1;
        for (int i = 1; i <= precision; i++)
            p = p * 10;
        return (Math.rint(d * p) / p);
    }
```

The for loop results in `p` containing 10 raised to the power contained in `precision`. The type `long` is used instead of `int` to allow the larger values of `p` that occur when 10 is raised to a power like 7 or 8. Also, it is not clear if `Math.pow(10.0, precision)` would yield exactly the correct value, although it would probably work just fine. So, `d*p` moves the decimal to the right `precision` places.

The `Math.rint` method rounds a double to the nearest integer that has a 0 for its fractional part. So `Math.rint(2.67)` is `3.0`. The division by `p` gets the return value back to the correct magnitude (shifting the decimal point back to the left).

JavaDoc—Creating Well-Documented Code[1]

We have been using comments in our code for help in documenting some basic programming decisions. Professional programmers create code that others may wish to use without having access to the source code. (Often, the compiled class files are distributed, while the .java files are proprietary.) To use another's methods or classes one needs access to the documentation.

JavaDoc is a tool that comes with the Java Development Kit from Sun Microsystems. A programmer can insert informative comments in a program, and the JavaDoc executable can extract the comments and create a Web page that documents the class and methods of the program. The Web pages become the documentation needed by others who use the methods and classes.

Java Comments

Java has three types of comments:
- "to end of current line" comments are indicated by `//`
- single or multiple line comments start with the symbol pair `/*` and end with the symbol pair `*/`
- JavaDoc comments start with the symbol triple `/**` and end with the symbol pair `*/`

JavaDoc comments are really just special cases of the second comment form but they are the only type of comment that JavaDoc will pay attention to.

JavaDoc Style

The following code fragment shows how JavaDoc comments might appear. This is the class Die that is part of the LabPkg package.

```
/**
 * A class that represents an N-sided die where N >=1 and when rolled any
 * side may come up on 'top' with the same probability.
 * @author J. F. Kent
 * @version 1.0, 3 Mar 1997
 * Copyright 1997
 */
public class Die
{
    private int numberOfSides;
    private int faceValue;
    private Random r;               // a random number generator
```

---

1. Use of JavaDoc is not critical for learning the Java language, but it is important for those who will work professionally with Java.

```
/**
 * Constructor.
 * @param n number of sides
 */
public Die(int n) {
    r = new Random(); // no explicit seed. It uses system time.
    numberOfSides = n;
    faceValue =
       (new Double(r.nextDouble() * numberOfSides)).intValue() + 1;
}

/**
 * Constructor.
 * @param n number of sides
 * @param seed value to initialize random number generator
 */

public Die (int n, long seed)
{
    r = new Random(seed);
    numberOfSides = n;
    faceValue =
       (new Double(r.nextDouble() * numberOfSides)).intValue() + 1;
}

/**
 * returns current 'top' value or face value of die
 */
public int valueOf()
{
    return faceValue;
}

/**
 * initiates a 'roll' or 'toss' of the die and obtains a possibly
 * new face value
 */
public void roll()
{
    faceValue = (new Double(r.nextDouble() * numberOfSides)).intValue() + 1;
}
}
```

Notice that at the beginning of the class there is a JavaDoc comment describing the class with appropriate information about the author and version. Then prior to each method is another JavaDoc comment describing the method.

JavaDoc recognizes several key symbols and words within the comment. They all start with the special symbol @.

- @author—author information
- @version—version number and date
- @param *parameter name*—information about the parameter
- @return—information about the return value

There are a few others, but these are the most common. In a post-lab exercise you will use JavaDoc to create a Web page for the Toolbox class. **As you create each method in the class you should provide a JavaDoc comment.**

All the Web pages for classes in the packages java.lang, javax.swing, and so on were created with JavaDoc. Object-oriented programs become self-documenting when the programmer inserts JavaDoc comments as she or he creates the code.

Review Questions	1. What is a method?
	2. How can you distinguish between a function and a procedure in the header line for a method?
	3. What is a parameter?
	4. Why are some methods static?
	5. Indicate the three forms comments can take in Java.

The Laboratory

Objectives	▪ To gain additional skill in the creation, testing, and use of methods.
	▪ To create a collection of static methods that can be used whenever you are developing a program.
	▪ To use JavaDoc-style comments to document methods.

A Guide to the Laboratory	▪ Download the two files `Toolbox.java` and `TBTest1.java` to your `labs` folder.
	▪ Task 1 requires that you compile the two files and run `TBTest1`. This is a simple example of how a method might be tested after it is written. There is nothing to turn in from this task.
	▪ Before completing the remaining tasks, which require you to write methods and test them, you will add code to define the values LEFT, RIGHT, and CENTER.
	▪ Task 2 requires that you complete a method `spaceStr` and test it. Be sure to include the JavaDoc comment. Print out and turn in a copy of your test program TBTest2.java.
	▪ Task 3 requires that you write the method `formatStr` and test it. Turn in a copy of your test program TBTest3.java. Don't forget the JavaDoc comments.
	▪ Task 4 requires that you write `formatInt` and test it. *Hint:* Consider converting the integer to a string and using `formatStr`. Add a JavaDoc comment. Turn in a copy of your test program TBTest4.java.
	▪ The final task is to use copy/paste/modify to create `formatDouble` and test it. Turn in the test program TBTest5.java.
	▪ Turn in a copy of Toolbox.java with your name(s) on it.
	If you get tasks 2 and 3 correct, the other two tasks will be very short.

Task 1	In your IDE's editor open the file `Toolbox.java`, which is shown below. We have used JavaDoc style comments, which will allow us to create HTML documentation for the class.

```
// Toolbox.java
// imports next if needed

/**
```

```
 * A class of static methods that provide a number of useful operations.
 * @author YOUR NAME
 * @version 1.0   DATE HERE
 */
public class Toolbox
{
    // no data components or constructors

    /**
     *  rounds a given double to a specific number of decimal places.
     *  If the precision exceeds 8, the original value is returned.
     *  @param d - the double value to be rounded
     *  @param precision - an integer in the range 0 to 8 indicating how many
     *   digits to the right of the decimal place should be kept. The
     *   right-most digit is rounded.
     */
    public static double roundDouble(double d, int precision)
    {
        if (precision < 0 || precision > 8)
        {
            return d;
        }
        else
        {
            long p = 1;
            for (int i = 1; i <= precision; i++)
            p = p * 10;
            return Math.rint(d * p) / p;
        }
    } // end of roundDouble

} // end of Toolbox class
```

Be sure to edit it to use your name and today's date. Then save the changes and compile it. There should be no errors.

Testing

You will use these methods in many programs so it is important that they are fully tested. Each method requires its own test program. The following test program was downloaded from the files page for this lab. It is called TBTest1.java.

```
// TBTest1.java
import LabPkg.*;

public class TBTest1
{
    public static void main(String[] args)
    {
        ViewFrame vf = new ViewFrame();
        vf.setVisible(true);
        vf.setIOEcho(true);

        double x = vf.readDouble("Enter a floating point value");
        for (int i = 0; i <= 10; i++)
        {
            vf.println("" + Toolbox.roundDouble(x,i));
        }
    }

}
```

Read it carefully. Do you understand what it would do if you were to run it and enter the value 4.50678125581011896?

Open it in the editor, compile it, and run it. A sample run is shown below. The entered value was echoed to the output window because we executed `vf.setIOEcho(true)`.

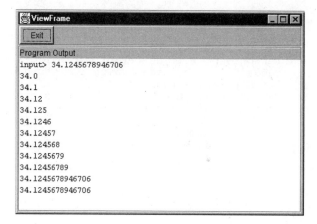

Notice that the value that was entered does round to 34 when precision is 0, but the output still shows it as a floating point value, 34.0.

The Other Tasks

For each of these tasks you are
- to write the specified method and add it to Toolbox.java, and then
- to write a simple test program. Name the test program according to the task number, for example, for task 3 call the test program TBTest3.java. The test program should fully "exercise" the method.

At the end of the laboratory you will be asked to turn in a printed copy of Toolbox.java and each of the test programs.

For each method you add to Toolbox you should provide a JavaDoc comment.

Before Going Further

You are to add three static integer variables to the class, as shown below:

```
public static final int LEFT = 1;
public static final int RIGHT = 2;
public static final int CENTER = 3;
```

They should be put at the beginning of the class before any methods. This means that they go on the line after the opening brace:

```
public class Toolbox
{
```

These are *named constants* and will be used as `Toolbox.LEFT` when calling the method described in task 3. The `final` adjective means that they truly are constants and cannot be changed.

No test program is required for this task, but you should recompile Toolbox.java to be sure that you didn't make any typographical errors.

Task 2

Write a method called `spaceStr` with the header

```
public static String spaceStr(int n)
```

where the method returns the empty string `""` if `n <= 0`. Otherwise it returns a string that contains n copies of the space character (the character you get when you type the space bar). The key idea is to declare a string w that is initially empty and then use a loop to concatenate n copies of the space character to it. Finally, return w.

Testing this is a little tricky as it is hard to count spaces visually on the screen. Consider code such as

```
vf.println("12345678901234567890");
vf.println("*" + Toolbox.spaceStr(7) + "*");
```

where vf is a ViewFrame object. The top line allows you to count characters more easily. You can get clever and use a loop with values from 0 to 20 to produce other versions of the second statement.

Put your test code in the file TBTest2.java and turn it in when the lab is completed.

Task 3

It is nice to be able to produce neat output, particularly in columns. This requires some effort because simple use of tab characters within a string doesn't always do the job. For example, if the following statement is in a loop

```
vf.println(name + "\t" + age);
```

where name is a string and age is an integer, and the names are "Joe" and "Florence", both with ages 25, the output is likely to be

```
Joe     25
Florence        25
```

because the normal tab stop is every seven characters. This problem could be solved if the name string were padded with space characters so that the resulting string was 12 characters long.

You are to write a method called formatStr that will take three parameters:

- a string object that is to receive padding with space characters
- an integer representing the desired new string length, including the padding
- an integer that must be one of Toolbox.LEFT, Toolbox.RIGHT, or Toolbox.CENTER and specifies where within the padded string the first parameter is placed (this indicates whether the first parameter is to be left-justified, right-justified, or centered in the resulting string).

If the second parameter is less than or equal to the length of the first parameter, the first parameter is returned unpadded.

The method's header line would look like

```
public static String formatStr(String s, int size, int justification)
```

There is a minor decision to be made if centering is specified and the number of padding spaces is odd. Put the extra space character after the string that is being padded.

In your test program you could put code like

```
for (int i = 1; i <= 3; i = i + 1)
{
    String s = vf.readString("Enter a word");
    vf.println("" + Toolbox.formatStr(s,10,Toolbox.LEFT));
    vf.println("" + Toolbox.formatStr(s,10,Toolbox.RIGHT));
    vf.println("" + Toolbox.formatStr(s,10,Toolbox.CENTER));
}
```

This produces output like that in the window below where we echoed the three input strings. Notice that we have strings of both odd and even lengths.

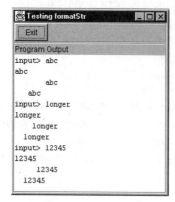

Task 4

A similar problem to that described in the previous task occurs when trying to display integers that are of differing numbers of digits. The default is to left-justify the value so that 20875 and 56 would appear as

```
20875
56
```

If you knew that the biggest value had six digits you might want to right-justify the values when displaying them.

You are to write a method `formatInt` that will have three parameters:
- an integer value that is to be formatted
- the size of the field in which the integer is to appear
- the code for the justification

This method returns a string containing the justified integer value. We easily convert the integer n to a string with `" " + n`. Then we can use the method of the previous task to do the work.

The header line would look like

```
public static String formatInt(int n, int size, int justification)
```

Hint: Consider converting the integer to a string and using the previous method.

Task 5

Write a method `formatDouble` that is similar to the `formatInt` method except it takes a double as its first parameter. Don't forget to turn in a printout of Toolbox.java and your test program files.

A Final Step

If you worked with a partner on this lab, it is important that both of you have a copy of Toolbox.java in your personal accounts. One easy way is to copy it onto a floppy disk. Then it can be copied by the partner whose account was not used during the lab.

Post-Laboratory Exercises

Exercise 1

Write a program that displays the square roots of the first 25 integers rounded to four decimal places. Use a neat column format with the original number in one column and the square root in another column. Make the columns 10 characters wide.

Exercise 2

Write a program that reads in a string like a sentence from the user and uses a StringTokenizer to break it into parts. Display each token and its length on a line in two columns. Each value should be right-justified in its column. Use 15 for the widths of the two fields.

Exercise 3

Write a method `roundDoubleToString` that converts a double to rounded form using roundDouble, and then converts the result to a string so that it displays trailing zeroes if necessary. For example, if the value is 34.56, then roundDoubleToString(34.56, 4) should return "34.5600". .

Exercise 4 (optional)

There are a number of situations in programming simulators or compilers when numbers need to be converted into their binary version. Binary means base 2. It uses only the symbols 0 and 1 to represent numbers. The number 5 in base 10 is written as 101 in base 2.

Numbers may be presented in various "bases." These are just different ways to express the same value. We always use a positional number system. The decimal value 2,563 is really

$$2*10^3 + 5*10^2 + 6*10^1 + 3*10^0$$

where we recall that 10^0 is just 1. In decimal or base 10 we have 10 symbols to work with: 0, 1, 2, 3, 4, 5, 6, 7, 8, and 9. In base 2, we only have 0 and 1.

In base 2, or binary, the value 110101 is short for

$$1*2^5 + 1*2^4 + 0*2^3 + 1*2^2 + 0*2^1 + 1*2^0$$

Some arithmetic shows that this is $32 + 16 + 0 + 4 + 0 + 1$, or 53, in base 10.

There are a number of issues that come up when considering numbers with signs, so we will consider only unsigned integers, i.e., integers with values greater than or equal to zero.

If you have an unsigned integer, how can you come up with the binary form? The easiest way is via a simple algorithm that uses a loop. We will construct the representation as a string of a specified length using the characters `'0'` and `'1'`. If the length is 10 and the binary value would be 110101, then it is written with leading zeroes as "0000110101". If the length is 4 and the binary value would be 110101 we would lose leading digits and get "0101". The algorithm is outlined below.

- Let S be the empty string initially.
- Let n be the decimal value (it must be $>= 0$).
- Let p be the number of positions.
- Repeat the following steps p times:
    - If n%2 is 0, then add the character '0' to the front of S. Otherwise, add the character '1' to the front of S.
    - Replace n by n/2.

When the algorithm is over, S holds the binary string.

You are to write the function `unsignedIntToBinaryStr` that will have two parameters:

- an integer that must be $>= 0$
- an integer that specifies the length of the desired binary string

The header will look like

```
public static String unsignedIntToBinaryStr(int n, int p)
```

n is to be written as a binary string of length p. If p is too small, only the right-most p digits will result.

One test program might display the first 60 integers in decimal and binary, using values of p like 4, 5, and 10. This could be done in four nice columns using some of the previous methods of this laboratory.

Exercise 5 (IDE-specific)

You are to create the JavaDoc documentation for Toolbox.java. This is easily done in the Kawa IDE. (If you are not using Kawa, check the documentation for your IDE to see if it can run the JavaDoc software.) First you must specify some options. Before doing that we suggest you create a folder called docs inside the folder containing your Toolbox.java file using Windows Explorer. This folder will be where JavaDoc will place the documentation.

In Kawa select Customize>Project Root Options, and then click on the JavaDoc tab. A sample pop-up window is shown below. You will need to

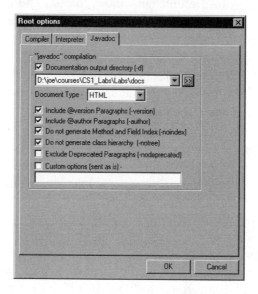

set the documentation output directory as the docs directory you just created and be sure the other boxes are checked.

Now you can close the options window and open Toolbox.java in the editing window. On the Build menu select JavaDoc (Build>JavaDoc). This creates the documentation.

Using Windows Explorer, find and open the docs folder and double-click on the file Toolbox.html to open it in Netscape or Internet Explorer. This page documents your class. Print out a copy of it from Netscape or IE.

Final Comments

You will be adding methods to this toolbox in later labs. You will be expected to use these methods in assigned programs. Feel free to add your own methods when you have a need to do so. Just remember that such methods should be applicable in more than a single program.

When you submit assignments that make use of the Toolbox class, please remember to turn in a copy of the Toolbox class so your assignment can be tested with your methods.

LABORATORY 8

Collections

There are many problems where *lists of values* need to be retained and processed several times. If all the values in a list are of the same type then one can use an array or a Vector object. Both maintain a linearly ordered collection of values with simple means of accessing the values. They differ in two fundamental ways:

- an array has a fixed size that must be known when it is declared, while a Vector object can expand automatically to accommodate new values
- a Vector is an instance of the Vector class, while an array is a language-supported organization of data in memory

All modern programming languages support arrays. Any object-oriented language either provides a class like Vector or allows you to write your own.

This laboratory will focus on problems that involve lists implemented as arrays. Vectors are discussed in the post-laboratory reading.

Pre-Laboratory Reading

The Need For Linear Collections (Lists)

Consider the following problems:

- A teacher would like a grade book program. The program would naturally have a list of CourseSection objects, and each of these CourseSection objects would have a list of Student objects. Both lists are linear collections. The list of Student objects is probably maintained in alphabetical order by name.

- A program is to have the user enter a list of values at the keyboard and then display the values in sorted order, or display the median if the values are numeric.

- A program is needed for a personal address book primarily containing names and telephone numbers. The records must be maintained so that efficient lookup is possible.

We can easily think of many other examples where lists are used in programs. Both arrays and vectors provide simple ways to implement lists.

There are programs that involve lists but don't require that the list be stored in memory. For example, consider a program that asks the user to enter a list of numeric values. When the entry of values is complete, the program displays the sum of the values or the largest value entered. It is possible to save the values in an internal list, but it is wholly unnecessary!

What Is "Sorted?"

"Sorted" means "in order by value." There are natural orders among numbers—increasing and decreasing orders. Similarly for text strings or simple words, we can order them lexicographically, i.e., by "dictionary order." For words we normally use alphabetical order, which is really just a simple name for lexicographical order. A dictionary can be viewed as a list of words maintained in alphabetical order.

There are items that cannot be naturally ordered in a complete sense. Consider pairs of numbers (x,y) that are points on a canvas. If one says that (a,b) <= (c,d) means a <= c and b <= d, then what about (2,5) and (3,3)? These two points are not comparable using this ordering. This type of order is said to be a partial order. We will not be concerned with these types of orderings.

Array Basics

An array is a block of allocated memory cells with a common name, all holding the same type of data. Each cell is referenced using its position within the block. Positions go from 0 to 1 less than the "length" of the block. As the term "block" implies, the cells are allocated contiguously.

The size of an array is the number of cells in the array. If x is the name of the array, then x.length will be the number of cells. Notice that this is like a data component reference rather than a method reference, which is used in the String class.

The characters [] after a type name signal an array of that type. We reference a particular item in the array x with x[position] where position is the "index" of the item within the block. As we said above, positions start at 0.

Declarations

Recall that when we want to use a variable to store a value, we must first declare the variable, then provide it with an initial value. We must go through a similar process in order to use an array to store a sequence of values. Here is how we declare a reference to an array:

```
int [] grades;   // create a reference to an array of ints
```

The second stage is the actual creation of the array, which involves setting aside enough memory for the number of items we want to store. We do this using the new keyword:

```
grades = new int[40];// allocate an array of 40 integers
```

This creates a memory area large enough to hold 40 int values, and makes grades refer to it. Since it seldom makes sense to create a reference to an array without setting aside memory for storing the array, we often combine these two statements:

```
int[] grades = new int[40]; // declare and allocate an array of
                            // 40 integers
```

For purposes of backward compatibility with similar programming languages, we can also use the following form to declare an array:

```
int grades[] = new int[40]; // equivalent to the declaration above
                            // but not preferred
```

Notice that the [] may be associated with the name or the type. (C++ uses the latter form only.) Also note that the allocation of space for the array does not provide it with initial values. That can be done by assignments like

```
grade[3] = 87;
```

or by setting all values initially to 0 like

```
for (int i = 0; i < 40; i++)
{
    grade[i] = 0;
}
```

Declarations with Initializations

It is possible to combine initialization and declaration, but in practice this is only done for small arrays.

```
String[] words = {"hello", "help", "hi", "hop"};
    // allocates an array of four strings and initializes it
```

In this type of declaration the allocation of space for four items is automatic.

Array Size

For an array x the integer value x.length holds the allocated number of elements of the array, even if not all items have been initialized. Do *not* confuse this with the length() method of the String class! The concepts are the same, but one is a method and the other is a data component.

Array Parameters

Arrays may be passed as arguments to functions that declare an array type parameter. It is not necessary to pass the size of the array as one can always check the value of the length data component. For example, suppose we wanted to find the largest value in an array of integers. We might use a function like that below:

```
public static int BiggestInArray(int[] list)
{
    int biggest = list[0];
    for (int i = 1; i < list.length; i++)
    {
        if (biggest < list[i])
        {
            biggest = list[i];
```

```
            }
        }
        return biggest;
    }
```

Notice that we use `list.length` to determine how many items are in the array list. The positions are 0 to `list.length - 1`.

We are implicitly assuming that the array being passed has been initialized.

A Sample Program

Consider a program that will ask the user to enter five words at the keyboard and then will display the words in reverse order of entry.

```
// ArrayDemo.java
// Program to read in five words and display them in the reverse
// order of their entry.

import LabPkg.*;

public class ArrayDemo
{
    public static void main(String[] args)
    {
        ViewFrame vf = new ViewFrame("ArrayDemo");
        vf.setVisible(true);

        String[] words = new String [5]; // the declaration
        for (int i = 0; i <= 4; i++)
        {
            words[i] = vf.readString("Enter a word"); // filling cell #i
        }
        for (int i = 4; i >= 0; i--)
        {
            vf.println(words[i]);  // printing out cell #i
        }
    }
}
```

The array name is words. It is declared to be of length 5. The two for loops use positions 0, 1, 2, 3, and 4, although not in the same order.

An Aside: Exchanging Values

We often must rearrange the values in an array if we want the values to be in sorted order. This is done by exchanging the contents of two cells at a time. This is called a "swap" operation.

Consider two integer variables x and y as declared below.

```
int x = 7;
int y = 5;
```

We visualize two locations in memory.

An exchange or swap would put the value 7 in the box for y and put the value 5 in the box for x. This can be done by assignment statements. But that requires a third box or else a value will be lost. (Try to complete the exchange just using x, y, and assignments and note what happens!)

Call the third box temp and initialize it to the value of x.

```
int temp = x;
```

Now the picture looks like

x [7]   y [5]   temp [7]

The code to finish the exchange is

```
x = y;        // x gets the value in y
y = temp;     // y gets the value in temp
```

Trace the result of these two steps in the picture above.

Exercise

Write the statements that would exchange the contents of the i-th and j-th cells of an array A. Assume the array holds String items.

Review Questions

1. What is an array?

2. What are the restrictions on arrays?

3. Assuming an array x of String objects, how would you refer to the item in position 2 of x?

4. How do you find the size of an array if the array is passed to a method as a parameter?

5. Assuming an array `numbers` of integers, write code that will display the integer values one per line starting with the value in position 0.

6. Write code that will find the smallest value in an array A of integers and print out its value.

7. Rewrite the code in the previous question so that we print out the position of the smallest value in A. Don't worry about duplicates—assume that all values are distinct.

The Laboratory

Objectives

- To use arrays in simple programs.
- To add some functions to your Toolbox class that have array parameters.

A Guide to the Laboratory

- Tasks 1 and 2 create a program and then modify it. Print out copies of each version to turn in.
- Tasks 3–9 ask you to write some methods that use arrays. These will go in your Toolbox.java file. There are really only three methods:
  - positionOfMax
  - swap
  - linearSearch

  but each one has a version for int and double types. **You must write a simple test program for each method.**

  Turn in a copy of Toolbox.java plus a copy of each test program.

Task 1

Write a program that will read in 10 integers and save them in an array. Then display only the values that are odd in reverse order of their entry. Call the program file `OddReverse.java`. When the program is working, print out a copy to turn in.

Task 2

Modify the previous program so that it will initially ask how many values will be entered and then create an array of the appropriate size. The rest is the same. Print out a copy of the working version.

Comment on Tasks 3–9

Each of these tasks asks for you to write a method to add to your Toolbox class. Please document each one using JavaDoc comments and write a short test program.

Task 3

Write a method called `positionOfMax` that will be added to your Toolbox class. Its header line will look like

```
public static int positionOfMax(int[] A, int first, int last)
```

The method will return the *position* of the largest value of A[first], A[first + 1], . . ., A[last]. We assume that first <= last and that both first and last are legal positions in the array A.

Task 4

Within the class Toolbox make a copy of the method above (use copy/paste), then modify your copy so that the parameter A has the declaration `double[]` A. **Java can distinguish among methods with the same name that have different parameter types.** This is called *polymorphism*—multiple names—and works because at least one of the corresponding parameters of the methods are different types.

Be sure that variables that refer to values in A rather than positions are also changed to type double. Of course, positions are still integers!

Task 5

Write a method called `swap` that will be added to your Toolbox class that will exchange the values in two array positions. The header line would be

```
public static void swap(int[] A, int i, int j)
```

and it would exchange A[i] and A[j]. We assume i and j are legal positions of the array.

Task 6

Write a version of the previous method for an array of double values. Use the copy/paste/modify method described in task 4.

Task 7

Write a version of the previous method for an array of type `Object`. Test this using an array of String objects.

Task 8	The most common operation on a list is a lookup to see if a value is found. The usual convention is to return the first position in which the value is found. If the value is not found, then usually we return -1, which cannot be a legal position. This is the common convention used by many programmers.

If there are no assumptions about the array, then a lookup must use the *linear search algorithm*. This is simple. We start at the first position and examine it to see if it is what we seek. If it is, we return that position number. Otherwise we go to the next position in the array and examine it. Essentially, we move down the line looking for our value. (In another lab we will see that if the array is sorted, there is a quicker way to search for a value.) If you reach the end of the array without finding your value, then -1 is returned.

Add to your Toolbox class the method

```
public static int linearSearch(int[]A, int first, int last,
                               int special)
```

where `special` is looked for in the array A[first], A[first + 1], . . ., A[last] and we assume `first <= last`. If `first > last`, return -1, and return -1 if `special` is not found. Otherwise return the position where `special` is first discovered.

Warning: Be careful *not* to assume first is 0 and last is A.length-1.

Task 9	Repeat the previous task but for an array of double values and a `special` of type double. Again use the copy/paste/modify method of task 4.

This ends the additions to Toolbox.java. You should have tested them all. You should close the file.

Post-Laboratory Reading and Exercises

Array Exercises

Exercise 1	Suppose you are given a sorted array A of double values. Write code that will display the median of the values in the array. The median value is the "middle" value if there are an odd number of values. If there are an even number of values then the median if the average of the two value on either side of the place where the array would be cut in half.

Put your code into a method called `getMedian` and add it to your Toolbox class. Test it with arrays that have an odd number of values and arrays that have an even number of values. **Be sure the arrays you use for testing are in sorted order.**

Exercise 2	An array is said to be symmetric if it is the same when its values are listed from first to last position and from last to first position. Add the following method to Toolbox and test it:

```
/**
 * @param A is an array of integer values
 * returns true if A is symmetric and false otherwise
 */
public static boolean isSymmetric(int[] A)
```

```
        {
            ...
        }
```

The Vector Class

The Vector class is part of the `java.util` package, so you will have to have

```
import java.util.*;
```

in your file.

A Vector object maintains a block of memory cells that can hold items of type Object. Hence, the cells can hold any type that is a direct or indirect extension of the Object class. For example, String is a class that extends Object so String objects can be placed in the cell of a vector object. When we retrieve a value from a cell in a vector object, what we get is an Object reference. Before using this reference, you must *typecast* it to a reference of the appropriate type. We will see how to do this in a moment. (If you decide to mix objects of differing types in the same vector, you must be able to decide what sort of an Object reference you get from the Vector really refers to. We shall come back to this.) Unfortunately, this generality excludes the Vector from holding primitive types like int and double. There is a way around this drawback, which we will discuss in the section "Wrapper Classes."

Just as with arrays, the block of cells maintained by the Vector object allows access by position, although methods must be used to do the access instead of the `[]` notation.

The main advantage of a Vector is that it does not require its size to be fixed. Initially there is a default size and when the Vector becomes full, the size is automatically increased to allow more cells at the end of the block. The method `size()` returns the current number of items in the Vector object—not the number of cells allocated!

Before looking at the methods of the Vector class, let's consider a simple example.

A Simple Vector Example

We will write a program that will ask the user to enter words one at a time and enter the special word "QUIT" to mark the end of the list. Then the program will display the list of words in the reverse order in which they were entered. Vector is useful here because

- the size is unknown
- the data consists of String objects instead of primitive values

The program is shown below. It is available for downloading if you want to compile and run it.

```
// VectorDemo.java
// Program to read in words, stopping when "QUIT" is entered,
//  and display them in the reverse order of their entry.

import LabPkg.*;
import java.util.*;

public class VectorDemo
{
    public static void main(String[] args)
    {
        ViewFrame vf = new ViewFrame("ArrayDemo");
        vf.setVisible(true);

        Vector words = new Vector(); // the declaration
```

```
    String s = vf.readString("Enter a word");
    while (!s.equals("QUIT"))
{
        words.add(s);   // appends s to the end of the vector's list
        s = vf.readString("Enter a word");
}

    int last = words.size() - 1; // last position in vector's list
    String t;
    for (int i = last; i >= 0; i--)
    {
        t = (String) words.elementAt(i);
        vf.println(t);   // printing out cell #i
    }
    }
}
}
```

We have put the declaration of the Vector object words in bold as well as calls to its methods. It is important to note that when we obtain the object at position i in the list with words.elementAt(i), we must explicitly "cast" it to the String object that it really is before using it. The (String) expression is how an explicit cast to the String type is written.

Selected Methods

The Vector class has a number of methods, which can be reviewed in the online documentation. We will look at just a few that might be useful to us.

- clear()—empties the vector's list, making its size zero
- elementAt(int p)—provides a reference to the object in position p
- size()—returns the number of objects in the vector's list
- add(Object o)—adds the object to the empty cell at the end of the list, expanding the number of available cells if need be
- removeElementAt(int p)—deletes the object at position p from the list and automatically modifies the positions of items that follow it by decreasing them by 1
- insertElementAt(Object o, int p)—inserts the object at the position p, automatically adjusting the positions of the objects that were at that position or after that position by increasing their positions by 1
- setElementAt(Object o, int p)—replaces the object at position p with this new object
- firstElement()—returns a reference to the first object in the vector but does not remove the object
- lastElement()—returns a reference to the last object in the vector
- isEmpty()—returns true only if the vector has no objects, otherwise returns false

The following program uses many of these methods. See if you can trace the program and predict what will be displayed on output. You can check your answer by downloading, compiling, and running the program. But first try to guess the output!

```
// VectorMethodsDemo.java
// A vector holding String objects is modified using methods
// from the Vector class. Try to predict the output.

import LabPkg.*;
import java.util.*;

public class VectorMethodsDemo
{
    public static void main(String[] args)
    {
```

```
ViewFrame vf = new ViewFrame("Predict the output");
vf.setVisible(true);

Vector w = new Vector();
w.add("dog");
w.add("cat");
w.add("snake");
w.add("horse");
w.add("bear");

vf.println("------------");
for (int i = 0; i < w.size(); i++)
{
    vf.println((String)w.elementAt(i));
}

w.removeElementAt(2);
w.insertElementAt("Hog", 3);
w.removeElementAt(2);
w.setElementAt("pony", 2);
vf.println("------------");

String t;
for (int i = 0; i < w.size(); i++)
{
  t = (String)w.elementAt(i);
  vf.println(t);
}
w.insertElementAt("frog", 0);
vf.println("First is " + (String)w.firstElement());
    }
}
```

Exercise 3

Write a program that will read in words until the special word "QUIT" is encountered. Each word will be inserted into a Vector object so that the items in the Vector object are *in sorted order*. After all words are entered, display the Vector object's contents from front (position 0) to back. Call the program file `VectorSorted.java`.

Hint: Notice that if the Vector is empty the first insertion is trivial. After that the Vector is sorted and you are simply trying to put a new item in its proper place. This is done by starting at the last item and working towards the front until you find the proper position for the new item. Then it is inserted. The Vector method `insertElementAt` makes this straightforward. (You can start at the front and move towards the back if you prefer.)

Try this by hand before writing code. Use a sequence of words like

```
dog
cat
fox
car
eat
horse
boy
QUIT
```

The determination of the correct location of a new word requires a loop. Think about the stopping condition of the loop.

Wrapper Classes

As you know the Vector class cannot handle primitive types like int and double, but there is a way to take a primitive type and enclose it in an object. We use what is called a "wrapper" class. For example, the integer value 5 can be put into an Integer object (notice the case of Integer) with

```
Integer x = new Integer(5);
```

The value 5 can be later extracted with the method `x.valueOf()`. This is what must be done if you want to use primitive types with a Vector.

Exercise 4 Write a program that will read in five integer values and store them in a vector. Then display them in the reverse order of their entry.

---

instanceof

A Vector can hold any Object type. When a value is retrieved, it must be explicitly cast to the proper type before use. Suppose a Vector contains both String and Integer objects. How can we know which is which? Well, Java provides an operator `instanceof` that can detect the real type of an object. Consider the following code:

```
Object x = v.elementAt(2); // v is a Vector object
if (x instanceof Integer)
{
    Integer i = (Integer)x;
    ... // use of i
}
else if (x instanceof String)
{
    String s = (String)x;
    ...  // use of s
}
```

Exercise 5 Write a program that will use a Die object with two sides. Roll the die six times. If the Die's value is 1, add an Integer object with value 20 to a Vector object. If the value is 2, add a String object with value "TWO" to the vector. Then display the contents of the vector in reverse order. Call the program file `VectorMixed.java`.

Command Line Arguments[1]

During the entire semester you have seen an array parameter to `main`.

`public static void main(`**`String[] args`**`)`

We simply haven't had a need to use this feature. The name of the parameter is `args`. It is an array of `String` items. What are these items? Well, they are not always used or we would have had to deal with them earlier.

How do we get values in this array of String objects?

Command Prompt Window In your IDE, if you have a program with the main class `Simple` (in the file `Simple.java`), then when you ask the IDE to run the program, it actually runs the "command"

`java Simple`

You can do this manually using a command prompt window as follows:

- Select `Start>Programs>Command Prompt` under Windows NT or Windows 2000. (This is called the MS-DOS Prompt under Windows 95/98.)
- A command line window will open and you will probably get a prompt like

  `C:\Winnt>`

---

1. The material on command line arguments is optional, but may be needed in some programs.

You are now able to type commands like "dir" or "cd" or "java Simple," although the last command requires that the file Simple.class be in the current folder. The dir command lists the contents of the current folder or directory. It shows the files and subfolders. The cd command changes the current folder.

- Assume that the file Simple.class is in the folder Z:\lab_folders. Enter the following sequence of commands on a laboratory computer:

```
Z:                - makes Z: the active drive
cd lab_folders
dir               - lists the files & looks for
                      Simple.class
java Simple       - runs the program
```

Obviously this is more work than running the program from your IDE but it does allow us to demonstrate command line parameters. Consider what would happen if you entered the command

```
java Simple 45 12 78
```

The method main with the array parameter args now has values for args. The array args contains three strings: "45", "12", and "78" in positions 0, 1, and 2, respectively. This is a way to get information to main as you initiate the program. Using command line arguments in this way can avoid the need for a time-consuming dialog with the user to determine initial values for a program.

The program below shows a trivial use of command line arguments. Although the three values are echoed to the output area, the program also shows how integer and double values can be converted from the String format to the int and double values. This would be necessary if we wanted to do arithmetic.

```java
// File:CommandLineArgs.java
// Description: Simple demo of command line arguments passed to main

import LabPkg.*;

public class CommandLineArgs
{
    public static void main(String[] args)
    {
        ViewFrame vf = new ViewFrame("Command Line Arguments");
        vf.setVisible(true);

        if (args.length != 3)
        {
            vf.showWarningMsg("Usage: java CommandLineArgs " +
                    "name age gpa");
            System.exit(0);
        }
        vf.println("Name: " + args[0]);
        int age = Integer.parseInt(args[1]);
        vf.println("Age is " + age);
        double gpa = Double.parseDouble(args[2]);
        vf.println("GPA is " + gpa);

    }
} // end of class
```

This program is available for download, so compile it and then run it in a command prompt window with the command

```
java CommandLineArgs Fred 21 3.58
```

Try it again with

```
java CommandLineArgs Fred Jones 21 3.58
```

You will get an error because the program will expect "Jones" to be the age value. This can be fixed with the command

```
java CommandLineArgs "Fred Jones" 21 3.58
```

The quotations on the command line allow spaces within arguments.

Exercise 6

Write a program called `LeapYear.java` that expects a single command line parameter, which should be an integer. Typical commands that run the program are

```
java LeapYear 1900
java LeapYear 1992
java LeapYear 2003
```

The program will output the string "Is a leap year!" or "Is not a leap year!" according to whether the parameter is a leap year or not.

Recall that a year is a leap year in our current calendar system if it is after 1582 and divisible by 4, with the exception that if it is a century year (1600, 1700, etc.) it must be divisible by 400. So 1600 is a leap year but 1700 is not.

Test your program using the command prompt.

Final Comment

You might think that command line parameters are things of the past, but it is possible to include them when creating shortcut icons on the desktop. For example, if the Netscape program is run with the command line argument `-mail`, it runs the mail reader instead of the browser. The shortcut command is

```
C:\Program Files\Communicator\...\netscape.exe -mail
```

where we have omitted part of the full path to the Netscape executable file.

9

Drawing with Java

This laboratory will examine the Graphics class methods and apply them in creating classes that represent (and draw) various shapes and symbols. We can think of these classes as components of pictures that we would like to construct. A PictureCanvas class will be written to display our pictures.

The primary goal is the introduction of basic ideas in computer graphics—color, location of images within a window or on a screen, and drawing of basic shapes. We will be doing simple drawing, which is distinct from "rendering" pictures. The creation of realistic images that might be used in an animated film is too sophisticated for this introductory class.

There are many fundamental ideas of object-oriented programming that will be introduced via the examples in the laboratory—interfaces, polymorphism, and dynamic dispatch of methods. It is not critical that you fully understand them all at first. But they provide some idea of the power and sophistication of object-oriented systems.

Don't forget that all the documentation on standard Java classes is available online. The package that is central for this laboratory is `java.awt`. For example, if you want to see all the methods of `Graphics` you can easily look at the JavaDoc pages found online.

Pre-Laboratory Reading

Basics of the Coordinate System for Drawing

The computer display is considered to be a large window that is rectangular in shape. It contains a rectangular pattern of colored dots called "pixels" or "picture elements." Drawing consists of setting the colors of certain pixels. The number of possible colors that a pixel can be set to depends on hardware, e.g., the amount of video RAM on a video card, but at least 256 colors are always supported and most computers support millions of colors.

The resolution of a computer screen is based on the number of columns and rows of pixels. The minimal resolution on modern PCs is 640 by 480 and most computers have a resolution of 1,024 by 768. The product of the two numbers is the number of pixels.

Drawing any object using a method that interacts with the graphics systems of your computer requires that you specify the position of the object. For example, a method to draw a line requires that the starting and ending pixels be given.

How do we specify a pixel's location?

This question is often replaced by "How do we specify a point in the window?" because in practice the only points are pixels!

Answer: We use the pixel's horizontal and vertical offsets from the upper-left corner of the window (the screen). We show this below with a line from pixel (10,30) to pixel (50,30).

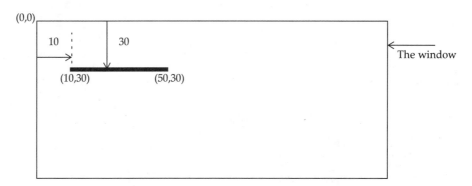

The general convention is that a point or pixel position (x, y) represents a horizontal offset from the left of an amount x and a vertical offset from the top of an amount y. For obvious practical reasons these should be non-negative integers. (It is possible to use floating point values, but pixels are actually at integral locations so some rounding or truncating will occur anyhow.)

The Graphics Class

A Graphics object is automatically associated with every visual component in Java. It contains the information needed to display colors, images, text, lines, and so on. In Java the Graphics class has many useful methods for drawing figures. Before we consider them, it will be useful to examine the Color class, because all drawing is performed by changing the color of pixels.

The Color Class

A Color object encapsulates information about a particular color. The usual context is RGB color definitions. RGB stands for red-green-blue. A color is defined by specifying amounts of these three basic colors. These three colors are used because they have been defined for computer displays in hardware. Each red, green, or blue color component is scaled from 0 to 255 (or from 0 to FF in hexadecimal[1] notation) or is given as a floating point value in the range 0.0 to 1.0. The Color class has constructors for both formats. The RGB triple of integers (255,255,255) is the same as the triple of floating point values (1.0,1.0,1.0) and represents white, while (0,0,0) represents black.

The Color class has 13 predefined Color values. They are static data members. Here are some examples:

```
Color.yellow
Color.white
Color.red
Color.cyan
Color.black
Color.darkGray
```

The code below shows how to create colors using the two types of RGB descriptions. There are four colors created and each is placed in a Vector object. An infinite loop (`while(true)`) is used to go through the four colors over and over again, setting the background of the canvas object to that color. We put a three-second delay between each color change. The initial color of the canvas is Color.yellow. An Iterator object is used to access the elements of the vector from first to last. This is discussed later in the pre-laboratory reading. (This file should be downloaded, compiled, and run. Modify it by adding some colors of your own. Also, you may want to change the delay from three seconds to only two seconds. You can stop the running of the program by killing the window.)

```java
// ColorDemo.java

import java.awt.*;
import LabPkg.*;
import java.util.*;

public class ColorDemo
{

    public static void main (String[] args)
    {
        Canvas c = new Canvas();
        c.setSize(ViewFrame.WIDTH, ViewFrame.HEIGHT * 3 / 4);
        c.setBackground(Color.yellow);
        Vector v = new Vector();
        // create some colors
        v.add(new Color(245,245,245)); // near white
        v.add(new Color((float)0.0, (float)0.0, (float)0.0)); // black
        v.add(new Color((float)1.0, (float)0.0, (float)0.0)); // red only
        v.add(new Color(50,50,200)); // a blue shade

        ViewFrame vf = new ViewFrame("ColorDemo", c);
        vf.setVisible(true);
        Useful.pause(15);

        while (true)    // you will need to kill the window to get out
        {
            Iterator i = v.iterator();
            while (i.hasNext())
            {
                c.setBackground((Color)i.next());
                c.repaint();
```

---

1. "Hexadecimal" refers to the base 16 number system, which is often used in programming because it takes an integral number of bits (four) to represent each digit in a hexadecimal number.

```
        Useful.pause(30); // wait three seconds
      }
    }
  }
}
```

We changed the background color of the canvas and then repainted the canvas. We could have changed the foreground color, which would change the color of text or lines drawn on the canvas.

Methods of the Graphics Class

The Graphics class has many methods for drawing common shapes like rectangles, ovals, and polygons, plus lines and text. An oval is really an ellipse, and a circle is an ellipse with special properties. For objects like rectangles you must either specify the four corner points or give the upper-left corner point and then the rectangle's width and length. If you take the former approach, you are thinking of the rectangle as a four-point polygon. The latter approach is normally used for rectangles.

A description of a few methods is given below. For the rest of the methods, refer to the online documentation for java.awt.Graphics.

- `drawString (String s, int x, int y)`—displays the string s starting at point (x, y) and using the current font and foreground color.
- `clearRect (int x, int y, int width, int height)`—essentially fills the rectangle with the upper-left corner at (x, y) and the specified width and height with the current background color.
- `drawLine (int x1, int y1, int x2, int y2)`—draws a line from (x1,y1) to (x2,y2).
- `drawRect (int x, int y, int width, int height)`—draws a rectangle with the upper-left corner at (x, y) and with the given width and height. Note that this draws the boundary of the rectangle. The next method draws a "solid" rectangle.
- `fillRect (int x, int y, int width, int height)`—draws a solid rectangle using the current foreground color.
- `drawOval (int x, int y, int width, int height)`—centers an oval in a rectangle with the upper-left corner at (x, y) and the specified width and height. If the rectangle is a square, this results in a circle.
- `fillOval (int x, int y, int width, int height)`—centers a solid oval in a rectangle with the upper-left corner at (x, y) and the specified width and height.
- `drawPolygon (int[] xpoints, int[] ypoints, int npoints)`—draws a polygon made up of lines connecting the points (xpoints[0], ypoints[0]), (xpoints[1], ypoints[1]), ... , (xpoints[npoints - 1], ypoints[npoints - 1]), and (xpoints[0], ypoints[0]). It is assumed that each array has at least npoints elements. The repeat of the initial point at the end automatically occurs so that the polygon is a closed figure. We could draw a triangle with vertices at (10,20), (60,20), and (25,50) with the code

```
int[] xCoord = {10,60,25};
int[] yCoord = {20,20,50};
g.drawPolygon(xCoord, yCoord, 3); //assumes g is
                                    a Graphics object
```

- `fillPolygon (int[] xpoints, int[] ypoints, int npoints)`—draws a solid, filled polygon bounded by lines connecting the points (xpoints[0], ypoints[0]), (xpoints[1], ypoints[1]), . . . , (xpoints[npoints - 1], ypoints[npoints - 1]), and (xpoints[0], ypoints[0]) using the current foreground color.

It is possible to draw "arcs," as well as rectangles with rounded corners. Drawing "rounded rectangles" (as the Java API documentation calls rectangles with rounded corners) is described later in the lab exercises.

An arc is really just a part of an oval. The starting and ending locations are given by angles. The value of 0 is at the 3 o'clock position while the value of 90 is at the 12 o'clock position. Positive angles are measured counterclockwise; negative angles are measured clockwise. The second angle is measured from the first angle. Hence, if the starting angle was 90 and the ending angle was -90, the arc would go from 12 o'clock clockwise to 3 o'clock.

The code below uses the `fillArc` method to visually count from 0 to 60, changing the arc's size once each second. Think of it as a simple timer. We make use of the `Useful.pause` method to delay for one second before redrawing the picture.

Download this program and run it to see these ideas in action. Don't worry about the details for now.

```
// CountUpTimer.java
// Illustrates use of some Graphics methods.
// Key is to display a "pie" that is proportional to the count from 0 to 60.
// The pie grows in size as each second goes by.

import java.awt.*;
import LabPkg.*;

public class CountUpTimer
{
    public static void main (String[] args)
    {
        Canvas c = new Canvas();
        c.setSize(ViewFrame.WIDTH, ViewFrame.HEIGHT * 2 / 3);
        c.setBackground(Color.yellow);
        c.setForeground(Color.red);

        ViewFrame vf = new ViewFrame("CountDownTimer", c);
        vf.setResizable(false);
        vf.setVisible(true);
        Graphics g = c.getGraphics();
        Useful.pause(20); // give ViewFrame a chance to draw itself
        Dimension d = c.getSize(); // we will want to center things
        int m = Math.min(d.width - 20, d.height - 20);
        int x = (d.width - 20 - m) / 2 + 10;
        int y = (d.height - 20 - m) / 2 + 10;
        for (int i = 0; i <= 60; i++)
        {
            vf.repaint();
            // now draw our figures
            g.drawRect(x,y,m,m);
            g.fillArc(x + 5,y + 5,m - 10,m - 10,90,-(int)(360 * (i / 60.0)));
            vf.println(""+i);
            Useful.pause(10); // wait one second
        }

    }
}
```

This illustrates the use of `drawRect` and `fillArc` methods. The Dimension class is in java.awt and has two public data members—`width` and `height`. We use the information on the size of the Canvas `c` to center our rectangle and arc.

Interfaces

Several times we have extended an existing class, particularly to create special canvas classes. Often we have a collection of classes that have a common *behavior*. In object-oriented programming jargon, the behavior is determined by a collection of methods and the list of these methods is called an interface specification. So another way of describing the similarities among the classes in our collection is to say that each of them has all of the methods in the interface specification. In Java terminology, we say that our classes *implement* the interface specification.

For example, we could define an interface called `Comparable` that had a single method

```
public int compareTo(Comparable otherObject)
```

The String class could be said to implement this interface because it contains the listed method. (The `Comparable` interface has been part of the java.lang package since version 1.2, and all of the wrapper classes for primitive types implement it.)

Consider the following interface specification, which we will use in the lab when we create picture components:

```
// PictureComponent.java
// interface definition
import java.awt.*;

/**
 * an interface used with drawable objects
 */

public interface PictureComponent
{
    /**
     * draw the object in outline form using g's current color
     * or the object's color if one was designated
     */
    public void draw (Graphics g);
    /**
     * draw the object in solid form using g's current color
     * or the object's color if one was designated
     */
    public void drawFilled (Graphics g);
    /**
     *  designate a color for the object to be used when drawing it
     */
    public void setColor (Color c);
}
```

We use the word "interface" instead of "class" and then list only the header lines of each method followed by a semicolon. This header line is called the *signature* of the method. These have been put in bold. The comments describe the generic behavior of each method.

Now if we were to create a class for a circle, the definition would look like

```
public class Circle implements PictureComponent
{
    // normal class stuff goes inside
}
```

By adding "implements PictureComponent" we signal to the Java compiler to look for the three methods.

Any object that implements a particular interface and then only uses the methods of the interface can be said to be of the type given by the interface. Look at the following, for example:

```
PictureComponent p = new Circle(...);
...
p.draw(...);
```

Notice that p has the type `PictureComponent` rather than `Circle`. In this context p cannot use any methods that are not in the interface list, even if the `Circle` class supplies other methods. It is interesting to note that we cannot actually create an object of type `PictureComponent`, because there are no definitions (method bodies) for the methods described by the interface. However, we can declare a reference variable, like p in the example, which has the type `PictureComponent`. Such a reference variable can then be used to refer to any object belonging to a class that implements the `PictureComponent` interface, such as `Circle`. We will see more of this in practice in the laboratory.

Note that a class may extend another class and also implement an interface:

```
public class Circle extends Oval implements PictureComponent
```

It is even possible for a single class to implement several interfaces. For example, if we wanted to be able to rank our Circle objects by size, we might declare the class as follows:

```
public class Circle extends Oval implements PictureComponent, Comparable
```

Iterator Mechanism

For arrays and vectors, we can process each of the items in order of position and be assured that we have seen all of the items. This is natural, because these particular data structures make their internal organization obvious to the user.

For objects that contain data items in a linear order, it is not always possible to refer to position. For example, in a *linked list* items are not in contiguous memory locations. Each item has a reference to the location of the item that follows it in the list. The object containing the linked list just has to have a reference to the first item's location. The order is linear but position cannot be used. How do we allow a user of the object to examine all of the items on the list in order? The answer is to use an *Iterator*. (In earlier versions of Java, this facility was referred to as an *Enumeration*.)

An Iterator object is an object that implements the Iterator interface. The two methods of this interface are

```
public boolean hasNext() - true if there are more items
                               to examine
public Object next() - returns the next item and
                          automatically advances the
                          implicit list position
```

An example of an Iterator is provided by the Vector class. The Vector method

```
public Iterator iterator()
```

allows the user to process all of the items in the vector without regard to their position. If vStr is a Vector object containing String objects, then the following code displays each item in the vector on the console screen:

```
Iterator i = vStr.iterator(); // get an Iterator object
while (i.hasNext())
{
    System.out.println((String)i.next());
}
```

As an example of how we might use this mechanism, suppose we were writing a program to play one of the card games in the solitaire family. If we were to create a class called CardPile for use in the game, we would not want to depend on whether the cards were maintained in an array or a vector or in a linked list when we displayed the cards on the screen. An Iterator object could be provided by the CardPile class as was done in the Vector class so that the cards would be accessed in the appropriate order for painting on the screen. This would allow us to change how we implemented our stack of cards without changing the code that displayed contents on the screen—a good design decision.

Summary Comment

Iteration is similar to linear search, but it is not an algorithm. It is a mechanism to access all the items in a (usually linear) collection.

The Laboratory

Objectives

- To gain experience using methods of the Graphics class.
- To create classes that have a visual component.
- To show how a collection of visual classes can be used to draw simple pictures using an interface definition and a vector's iterator.

A Guide to the Laboratory

- Of course, you will start by downloading the files used in the lab from the Web. First you will create a project called `Pictures` and add the file `PictureComponent.java` to it. Once it is compiled, the project will not have changed and can be closed.
- You will create and test the classes Circle, Rect, RoundedRect, and Triangle. Each of the classes represents a figure and may be drawn. You will turn in copies of each file plus the test program files. Triangle.java is the hardest. The others are simple but require the use of methods from the Graphics class.
- You will complete the file PictureTest.java that will draw a pattern using the classes above. This will be turned in.

Creating Picture Components

We want to create classes that correspond to the following shapes and objects:
- a circle
- a triangle
- a diamond, as on a playing card
- a rectangle
- a rectangle with rounded corners
- a heart, as on a playing card
- a spade, as on a playing card
- a club, as on a playing card

Each class will encapsulate the key information about the object—its location and size—and will have methods that draw the object. The drawing methods will be passed a Graphics object, which will perform the actual drawing. Each class will implement the PictureComponent interface described in the pre-lab reading. The last three tasks are more difficult and will be done in the post-laboratory section.

Preliminaries

You should have the IDE open and the project `Pictures` created. Be sure the project is in the same folder as the files you have downloaded for the laboratory.

The file `PictureComponent.java` contains the definition of the interface `PictureComponent`. (Look back at the definition of an interface in the pre-lab reading.) **Add that file to your project.** Open it and compile it. Once it is compiled, close that file, leaving the IDE open.

Task 1: The Circle Class

We wish to define a Circle class. We have to ask ourselves questions as we design the class:

- What data members will the class have?
  - What state must be maintained by the objects of the class?
  - Which data members should be public? protected? private?
- What methods will be required?
  - Constructors must be considered.
  - The "get/set" methods for accessing the data components.
  - Any interface requirements.
- Should the class be an extension of an existing class or simply a class that doesn't use inheritance?
- How will the class be used?

These are the fundamental questions for the creation of any new class that is not just a collection of static methods like your Toolbox class. The order in which you answer the questions will vary. For example, it is good to think about the use of the class first as that will help determine what methods might be needed. On the other hand, you must think about the information that the class encapsulates, as that determines the data members.

Think about the characteristics of a Circle object.

- It will be used in pictures displayed in a window on the screen.
- It needs a location.
- It needs a size.
- It may need a color.
- It should support the PictureComponent interface.
- There doesn't seem to be any existing class that it might extend. (There is no Oval class already defined.)
- It isn't necessary to make the data components public or protected, so probably consider them private for now.

These answers allow us to start naturally by creating the file `Circle.java`, shown below. It is not complete; two methods need filling in. Notice that the data member `color` is initially `null`, which means that it does not reference a Color object. It can get a value via a constructor or the `setColor` method.

```
// Circle.java
// Programmer(s):

import java.awt.*;

/**
 * representation of a circle that is drawable
 */
public class Circle implements PictureComponent
{
    // data components
```

```
// (x, y) is center of circle
private int x;
private int y;
private int radius;
private Color color = null;

// constructors
/**
 * center is specified by (xPoint, yPoint) and r is radius
 */
public Circle (int xPoint, int yPoint, int r)
{
    x = xPoint;
    y = yPoint;
    radius = r;
}


public Circle (int xPoint, int yPoint, int r, Color c)
{
    x = xPoint;
    y = yPoint;
    radius = r;
    color = c;
}

// methods
public void draw (Graphics g)
{

        ┌─────────────────────────────────┐
        │   fill this in                  │
        │                                 │
        │                                 │
        └─────────────────────────────────┘

}

public void drawFilled (Graphics g)
{
        ┌─────────────────────────────────┐
        │   fill this in                  │
        │                                 │
        │                                 │
        └─────────────────────────────────┘

}

public void setColor (Color c)
{
    color = c;
}

}
```

(You can download this partially completed file, add it to your project, and open it in the IDE's editor.) You will want to use `g.drawOval` and `g.fillOval` as you complete the two incomplete methods. But you need to be alert to whether the `color` data member is set or not. Thus, the form of your code looks like

```
if (color == null) // just let g use its color
{
    g.drawOval(...);
}
else // use the designated color value
{
    Color c = g.getColor(); // save g's original color
    g.setColor(color); // give it our color
    g.drawOval(...);
    g.setColor(c); // reset g's color back to its
                   // original value
}
```

Warning: Please look back at the description for `drawOval` in the pre-lab reading.

Complete the class file and compile it to check for errors. Download the test program `CircleTest.java` and add it to your project. Print out a copy and read it before compiling it and running the project. Can you predict where the circles will be drawn?

When things are working properly, print out a copy of the completed Circle.java to turn in and make sure your name is on it.

Task 2: The Rect Class

Java has a Rectangle class in version 1.2, which is an extension of Rectangle2D. We want to avoid confusion with that class (which doesn't have the methods we want to include), so we will call our class `Rect`.

We want a real rectangle and not a parallelogram or general four-point polygon. Hence, we will require that the user specify

- the coordinates of the upper-left corner and
- the width and height.

This is simple and consistent with how the Graphics class views rectangles.

You are to create a Rect class that implements the PictureComponent interface. It will be in the file `Rect.java`. You are to create a test file `RectTest.java` to see if it is working properly. You will need to *remove* the file `CircleTest.java` from the project before adding your two new files. Leave Circle.java in the project.

When things are working properly, print out copies of Rect.java and RectTest.java to turn in.

Task 3: The RoundedRect Class

We want to be able to draw a rectangle with rounded corners. The Graphics class has methods

```
public void drawRoundRect (int x, int y, int width,
                           int height, int arcWidth, int arcHeight)
public void fillRoundRect (int x, int y, int width,
                           int height, int arcWidth, int arcHeight)
```

where the `arcWidth` and `arcHeight` parameters are the *diameters* of the horizontal and vertical arc components, respectively, at each corner. In our rounded rectangle we will make both the horizontal and vertical arc components the same and use *radius* rather than diameter.

Obviously the radius cannot exceed one half the length of the smaller dimension of the rectangle. If a radius value is not specified, you are to set it to be the value of `(int)((0.1) * Math.min(width, height))`. Of course, when you draw the rounded rectangle you will use `2 * radius` for the two arc components in the methods above.

This means that you will actually need to write four constructors for RoundedRect: one that takes the rectangle dimensions only; one that takes the rectangle dimensions and a color; one that takes the rectangle dimensions plus the corner radius; and one that takes the rectangle dimensions, the corner radius, and a color. Here are the signatures for the various constructors:

```
public RoundedRect(int xPoint, int yPoint, int w, int h)
public RoundedRect(int xPoint, int yPoint, int w, int h, Color c)
public RoundedRect(int xPoint, int yPoint, int w, int h, int r)
public RoundedRect(int xPoint, int yPoint, int w, int h, int r, Color c)
```

The test program `RoundedRectTest.java` is simple and may be downloaded for your use after you create `RoundedRect.java`. You will need to remove the other testing programs (RectTest.java) from the project before adding RoundedRectTest.java.

Make sure your name is in a comment in RoundedRect.java and print out a copy to turn in.

Task 4: The Triangle Class

You are to create a class Triangle. Follow the model for previous classes but remember that a triangle is determined by three points.

The triangle drawing will use g.drawPolygon and g.fillPolygon, with three points specified. This means that the data components will need to be kept as two integer arrays of size 3 each, plus a Color variable.

Simply use

```
private int[] x = new int[3];
private int[] y = new int[3];
```

Then in the constructors you can have code like

```
public Triangle (int[] xpoints, int[] ypoints)
{
    for (int p = 0; p <= 2; p++)
    {
        x[p] = xpoints[p];
        y[p] = ypoints[p];
    }
}
```

Then a call to g.drawPolygon(x, y, 3) will draw your triangle.

As a convenience, we also want to be able to provide three points like (50, 12), (160, 80), and (80, 200) in the form

```
Triangle t = new Triangle(50,12,160,80,80,200);
```

This requires a constructor like

```
public Triangle (int x1, int y1, int, x2, int y2, int x3, int y3)
{
    // fill arrays x and y with the parameter values

}
```

Here are some examples of Triangles:

```
Triangle t = new Triangle(50,12,160,80,80,200);
Triangle s = new Triangle(220, 100, 220, 50, 50, 50, Color.blue);
int[] a = {100, 200, 150};
int[] b = {125, 10, 10};
Triangle u = new Triangle(a, b); // no color specified
```

In the last triangle the points are (100,125), (200, 10), and (150, 10).

You need four constructors:

- two arrays, no color
- two arrays, color
- six values of coordinates, no color
- six values of coordinates, color

You are to *remove* any of the previous test files from the project. Then create the file Triangle.java and a test program file TriangleTest.java. Add both files to your project. Compile everything and run the test program.

When things seem to be working properly, print out copies of Triangle.java and TriangleTest.java to turn in. Be sure your names are on them.

Task 5: The PictureCanvas Class and Creating a Picture

We have written the four classes
- Circle
- Rect
- RoundedRect
- Triangle

All may be considered of type `PictureComponent`, as they all implement that interface. We could have added other methods to each class. For example, we could have a method `setRadius(int r)` in the Circle class that would change the radius of the Circle object. We simply didn't want to take the time during the lab to do so, but such methods should be added if these classes are to be flexible in their uses.

You can draw a picture by creating a collection of PictureComponent objects and then calling their `draw` or `drawFilled` methods in sequence. It is important to note that when a component is drawn it obscures what is under it. Hence, drawing should be "bottom up."

We can create an extension of the Canvas class that will be given a vector of PictureComponent objects and will display them in sequence to create a picture or pattern whenever the canvas is repainted.

Recall that any resizing of a window calls the repaint method, which ultimately causes paint to be called. The paint method is what you must modify to create the special PictureCanvas. The code is shown below and may be downloaded and added to the project.

```java
// PictureCanvas.java
import java.util.*;
import java.awt.*;

/**
 * A Canvas extension that displays the contents of a vector
 * of PictureComponent objects to create a picture.
 */
public class PictureCanvas extends Canvas
{
    Vector pictureParts; // assume that it contains PictureComponent objects

    // constructor
    public PictureCanvas (Vector v)
    {
        super(); // calls the constructor for Canvas
        pictureParts = v;
    }

    /**
     * our paint method uses the vector of PictureComponents to construct
     * a picture by drawing each component in turn
     */
    public void paint (Graphics g)
    {
        Dimension d = getSize();
        g.clearRect(0,0,d.width,d.height);
        Iterator i = pictureParts.iterator();
        while (i.hasNext())
        {
            PictureComponent p = (PictureComponent)i.next();
            p.drawFilled(g);
        }
    }

}
```

Notice that the paint method uses an iterator over the elements of the vector to obtain the picture components and draw them. It uses only the `drawFilled` method of each object.

Your Task

Remove any previous test program files from the project. Your project should contain the files for the four classes Circle, Rect, RoundedRect, and Triangle, plus the files ProgramComponents.java and PictureCanvas.java.

You are to create a file `PictureTest.java`, which will draw the picture below. The picture was created by using a PictureCanvas as the Canvas part of a ViewFrame object. The window was resized to be smaller so that the output area was hidden. Because we can't show you this image in color here, we have

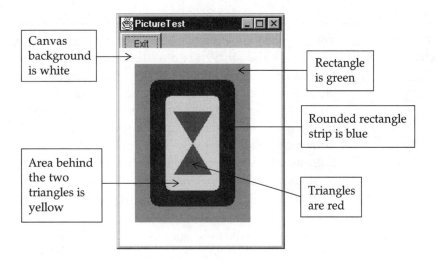

indicated the colors in the text callouts. The outside rectangle is 150 by 200 pixels. The green border that appears is 20 pixels wide, as is the blue one. The canvas has its size set to 300 by 250, although it could be narrower.

Some incomplete program code is shown below.

```
// PictureTest.java
// Name:
// We create a PictureCanvas object and show it in a ViewFrame.

import java.awt.*;
import LabPkg.*;
import java.util.*;
public class PictureTest
{
    public static void main (String[] args)
    {
        Vector p = new Vector();
        // create and add the PictureComponents to p
                // ----fill in----

        Canvas c = new PictureCanvas(p);
        c.setSize(300,250);
        c.setBackground(Color.white);
        ViewFrame vf = new ViewFrame("PictureTest", c);
        vf.setVisible(true);
    }
}
```

Complete the part to create the picture components and add them to the vector. The "Collections" laboratory has material about vectors, but this is a simple task. For example, if we wanted to create a Rect object and add it to the Vector object p, we would write

```
p.add(new Rect(10, 10, 100, 150, Color.red));
```

This Rect object would be located at (10,10), have a width of 100 and a height of 150, and be red.

Be sure to put the shapes in the correct order—the first component added to the vector will be the first one painted! It should be the "bottom" component.

You may want to play around with the sizes somewhat to get the picture to look nice. When the program is completed, print out a copy of the file PictureTest.java to turn in. You may want to show it to your lab instructor to check that it meets the criteria.

Comments on Key Ideas

You designed and created classes that implemented certain methods and thus all could be used in a certain context even though they were quite different in the state information they contained. The concept of an *interface* was used to illustrate that all these classes were drawable.

The PictureCanvas illustrates *inheritance,* as it extends an existing class. In that class we only define a constructor and redefine the `paint` method. The other methods of Canvas such as `setSize` and `setBackground` are automatically available, having been inherited from the Canvas class.

In the code above we have the line

```
Canvas c = new PictureCanvas(p);
```

c is declared to be a Canvas object but is created as a PictureCanvas object. This is fine if we use only methods of the Canvas class. But we have a `paint` method for Canvas and a `paint` method for PictureCanvas. When c is resized, which is used? The answer is the `paint` method for PictureCanvas. At run time the computer is able to determine that c is really an instance of PictureCanvas and calls the correct `paint` method. This is called *dynamic dispatch* and is critical in the implementation of object-oriented languages like Java, C++, and Smalltalk. Finally, we used an Iterator object to access the elements of a vector in order.

We are drawing pictures composed of simple elements. Real computer graphics is much more sophisticated, but some ideas still hold. Once you have developed skill with programming and have had some linear algebra (to help with image translations and rotations) you might want to take a computer graphics course to see how images like those in the movie "Toy Story" and "The Matrix" are created. Animations are just sequences of pictures painted 30 or more times per second. Once the pictures are available, the animations are not hard to implement.

Post-Laboratory Exercises

We would like to have classes that give us images for the four suits in a standard deck of playing cards—a diamond, a heart, a spade, and a club. You will develop these images (actually classes for the images) in this post-laboratory exercise. The images then can be used in a later project or laboratory to write a solitaire game.

We have one problem—we cannot draw a filled chord of a circle, a portion of a circle cut off by a line, without extremely tedious effort. This makes it difficult to draw the heart and spade as you normally would see them. We will make do with a crude rendition that suggests these images. The files `CardSuitSymbols.java` and `CardsCanvas.java` can be downloaded and added to your Pictures project. Remove any previous files in the project that contain a `main` method. Rebuild all and run the result after you have completed all the post-laboratory exercises. The result of running the program is shown below. This should help you visualize the images as you read the instructions. Notice that we don't bother to put six diamond symbols on the 6 of diamonds. These card images will work for now.

Exercise 1: Diamond

Create a Diamond class according to the description in the JavaDoc comment below.

```
/**
 * A diamond symbol is determined by a bounding rectangle
 * and has as its four points the midpoints of the four
 * sides of the rectangle. The rectangle is specified as
 * usual by its upper-left corner and its length and width.
 * Color may be designated or not. The current foreground
 * color will be used if no color is designated.
 */
public class Diamond implements PictureComponent
```

Notice that the class will implement the PictureComponent interface. You will want to think of this as a four-point polygon when drawing it.

As usual, after writing the class develop a test program to display several Diamond objects on a Canvas. Print out a copy of the file Diamond.java to turn in.

Exercise 2: Club

We will create a symbol for a club by using three circles and a triangle. The three circles are mutually tangent. The triangle is isosceles and extends downward from the lowest of the three tangent points. A crude picture is shown below. We show in dotted lines a rectangular region for the figure. The two key

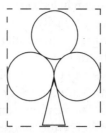

determining pieces of data that we will use to characterize this component are

- the point at the upper-left corner of the enclosing rectangle and
- the radius of the circles.

Then we will set the width of the rectangle to be 4*radius and the height to be the integer form of 4.7*radius. The 4.7 is really an approximation of the value of $3 + \sqrt{3}$ and was determined by plane geometry. The base of the triangle will have a length equal to the radius of the circle.

When you create the Club class you will have two constructors. The drawing will use three Circle objects and one Triangle object. An outline of the class is below.

```java
public class Club implements PictureComponent
{
    int x;
    int y;
    int radius;
    int width;
    int height;
    Circle cUp;
    Circle cLeft;
    Circle cRight;
    Triangle base;
    Color color = null;

    // constructors
    public Club(int xPoint, int yPoint, int r)
    {
        x = xPoint;
        y = yPoint;
        radius = r;
        width = radius * 4;
        height = (int)(4.7 * radius);
        cUp = new Circle(...);   // FILL IN THE PARAMETERS
        cLeft = new Circle(...);
        cRight = new Circle(...);
        base = new Triangle(...);
    }

    public Club(int xPoint, int yPoint, int r, Color c)
    {
        this(xPoint, yPoint, r);
        color = c;
    }

    public void draw(Graphics g)
    {
    }

    public void drawFilled(Graphics g)
    {
    }

    public void setColor(Color c)
    {
```

```
        color = c;
    }
}
```

When the class is written and compiled, write a test program to display some Club objects—filled and unfilled. Print out a copy of Club.java to turn in.

Exercise 3: Spade

We will render a spade as two triangles within a bounding rectangle. The smaller triangle will overlap the larger one by five pixels. A crude drawing illustrates our idea:

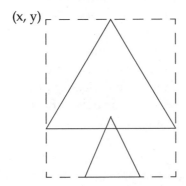

The top points of each triangle will be centered horizontally. The length of the base of the small triangle will be one third of the width of the bounding rectangle and will be centered. The two lower points of the large triangle will be located three quarters of the way down the sides of the bounding rectangle.

The visual image and its location will be determined entirely by the bounding rectangle's position and size and the conventions described above for the location of the two triangles within the rectangle.

Write the class Spade and test it. Print out a copy of Spade.java to turn in.

Exercise 4: Heart

This is the most difficult figure to approximate with lines. We will use a polygon within a bounding rectangle, i.e., all of the points of the polygon will be in terms of the width and height of the rectangle and the location of its upper-left corner. A crude picture gives the idea:

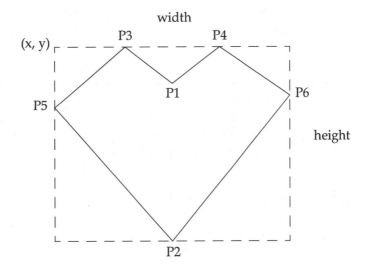

There will be six points that must be located. P1 and P2 will be centered horizontally. P2 will be the midpoint of the lower side of the bounding rectangle. P1 will be vertically displaced below the top side of the rectangle by an amount that is one fifth of the height of the bounding rectangle. P3 and P4 will split the top side of the rectangle in thirds. P5 and P6 will be one third of the way down the sides of the rectangle from the top. (You could probably do a more refined version with additional points or you could change the relative locations, but that is a creative decision—we still can't draw a filled chord which would be needed to round the sides properly.)

Create the Heart class with the constructors being passed the coordinates of the upper-left corner of the bounding rectangle, its width, its length, and (optionally) its color. After compiling the code and running a simple test program, print out a copy of Heart.java to turn in.

At this point, the files `CardSuitSymbols.java` and `CardsCanvas.java` can be downloaded and added to your Pictures project. Remove any previous files in the project that contain a `main` method. Rebuild all and run the result to be sure your classes are working properly.

Exercise 5: An Automotive Logo

Many automobile manufacturers use logos composed of just the simple elements we have created. An example is the Mercedes-Benz symbol. The Chrysler logo is another.

Select a logo and create a PictureCanvas instance that displays it. This means you have to construct the vector of PictureComponents needed. This is for fun.

Exercise 6: A Regular Hexagon

A regular hexagon has six sides, all of equal length. Games like Othello use a board of hexagons. If we wanted to display such a board we would need to be able to draw such figures.

Go through the design questions to determine what information would be needed to locate a hexagon and determine its size. Create a Hexagon class that implements PictureComponent.

Hint: A hexagon's corner points are six evenly spaced points on a circle. Specify the center of the circle (which is the center of the hexagon) and the distance from the center to a corner point, i.e., the radius of the circle. Then use basic trigonometry and analytical geometry to give the coordinates of the six points.

Postscript

We have been placing our pictures on Canvas objects that are part of ViewFrame objects. This is rather unsophisticated. We will see how to create windows with just a Canvas object and windows that are part of Web pages. A later lab on basic use of what is called the "AWT" will cover this topic.

LABORATORY 10

Recursive Methods

Recursion is the name given to the process whereby something is defined or expressed in terms of itself. For example, there is a special sequence of numbers called the Fibonacci sequence that is defined as follows:

- the first number in the sequence is 1
- the second number of the sequence is also 1
- the n-th number is denoted F(n), for n = 3, 4, 5, ..., and is defined by

```
F(n) = F(n - 1) + F(n - 2)
```

This last equation says that the n-th value is the sum of the preceding two values. The equation is said to be recursive because we define F in terms of itself.

While recursive definitions may seem strange, they are useful if stated properly. For example, if we did not know that F(1) and F(2) were both 1, then we would have a problem when calculating F(3). In this case we would say that the first and second values are the *base* values. Without such base values the definition is not sound.

The purpose of this laboratory is to explore and write recursive methods. Many algorithms are naturally stated in a recursive formulation and implemented using recursive methods.

Pre-Laboratory Reading

Recursion

A method is *directly* recursive if it calls itself. It is *indirectly* recursive if it calls another method, which then may call it. There may be any number of methods involved in indirect recursion. We will focus on direct recursion in this laboratory.

A simple example of (direct) recursion can be used to generate the value of n!, "n factorial." There are two ways to define n!. Both have 0! and 1! equal to 1 and indicate that n! is not defined for n less than 0.

The iterative way says that for n > 1,

```
n! = 1 * 2 * . . . * n
```

The recursive ways says

```
n! = n * (n - 1)!
```

Both yield the same value for n!, and they illustrate an important principle:

> Any task that can be done by iteration, can also be done via recursion and vice versa.

While this is a true statement in theory, in practice it is often hard to see how a recursive task can be done via iteration or vice versa.

The fact Method

The following example uses a static method `fact` to compute the factorial of its parameter. If you compile and run it, be careful to use reasonably small values, as numbers like 20! are quite large and 100! is too big for any computer to store. You might try running the program several times with a sequence of values like 5, 10, 15, and 20. You will get a negative result with 20! because the result is too large to store in the computer and the sign is modified.

```java
// FactorialDemo.java
// illustrates a recursive method to compute n!

import LabPkg.*;

public class FactorialDemo
{
    public static void main(String[] args)
    {
        ViewFrame vf = new ViewFrame("FactorialDemo");
        vf.setVisible(true);

        int x = vf.readInt("Enter a positive integer");
        if (x < 0)
        {
            vf.showWarningMsg("Negative values are not allowed.");
        }
        else
        {
            vf.println("" + x + "! is " + fact(x)); // fact is called here
        }
    }

    public static int fact(int n)
    {
        if (n == 0 || n == 1)
        {
            return 1;
        }
        else
        {
            return n * fact(n - 1);
```

```
        }
    }
}
```

Look carefully at the method `fact`. It has two parts, which correspond to the base cases and the recursive definition. We have boldfaced the key recursive step.

The part that makes the recursion correct is the base case where there is no recursion. This is when n is 0 or 1. The case of a negative value for n is not tested, as we are assuming `n >= 0`. We could have added that check within the fact method, but we opted to check that condition in `main`.

To help you understand how the method `fact` computes the correct value, fill in the table below using a trace of `fact`.

n	fact(n)
0	1
1	1
2	
3	
4	
5	
6	

Another Recursive Function

Consider the following recursive method, which may appear to be somewhat cryptic. Do you see the recursive call? What type of object is created and returned by the function?

```
public static String R(String s)
{
    if (s.length() == 0)
        return "";
    else
        return s.charAt(s.length() - 1) + R(s.substring(0, s.length() - 1));
}
```

Recall that `s.substring(0, s.length() - 1)` will be the string that is the same as s except without the last character. For example, `s.substring(5, 8)` will be the substring from position 5 through 7. Position 8 marks the position after the substring in this case.

By reading the method and tracing it, complete the table's missing values.

s	R(s)
""	""
"a"	'a' + "" = "a"
"ab"	
"abc"	
"abcd"	

After completing the table you should be able to see what the function is returning. Describe it.

A Recursive Procedure

The previous examples perform a computation or a construction and return values. Hence the methods are functions. Recursion is just as useful for procedures. Consider the algorithm below to sort an array A of values from position i to position j in ascending order. Normally, we assume i <= j.

SORT A from position i to position j:
- If i >= j, stop.
- Let p be the position of the largest value from A[i] to A[j].
- Swap A[p] and A[j] to put the largest value in the last position.
- Perform this algorithm on A from i to j - 1.

The last step is the recursive one. Once the largest value is in the last position, the other items of the array just need to be sorted. The procedure stops when there is at most one item to be sorted. This is when i >= j becomes true and represents the base case.

The code below will be put in your Toolbox class for sorting arrays of integers. It could be modified to sort double values. The procedure sorts A[first], A[first + 1], . . ., A[last].

```
public static void selectionSortRecursive(int[] A, int first, int last)
{
    if (first >= last)
    {
        return; // at most one item
    }
    int p = maxOnList(A, first, last);
    swap(A, p, last);
    selectionSortRecursive(A, first, last - 1);
}
```

The recursive step has been put in bold.

A test program is shown below. In the laboratory you will put the method in Toolbox and then run the test program. We are assuming that you completed the laboratory on arrays and vectors where you wrote the methods positionOfMax and swap.

```
// SortDemo.java
// Uses selectionSort method of Toolbox class to sort an integer array

import LabPkg.*;

public class SortDemo
{
    public static void main(String[] args)
    {
        ViewFrame vf = new ViewFrame("SortDemo");
        vf.setVisible(true);

        int[] nums = new int [7];
        for (int i = 0; i < 7; i++)
        {
            nums[i] = vf.readInt("Enter an integer");
        }

        Toolbox.selectionSortRecursive(nums, 0, 6); // sort entire array

        for (int i = 0; i < 7; i++)
        {
            vf.println("" + nums[i]);
        }
    }
}
```

| Hints for Writing Recursive Methods | The examples illustrate recursive functions and a recursive procedure, but you still must think in the correct way to write a recursive method. Here are some key steps: |

- Be sure there is a *base* or *stopping case* and make sure your code asks about it first. This case requires no recursion. For example, in the sorting procedure the stopping case is when there is at most a single element to consider.
- When you make the recursive call, be sure you are moving closer to the stopping case. In the sorting procedure, the array's final position that was being considered was modified by reducing it by one. This meant that the number of items to be arranged was one less than before. Hence the procedure was closer to having a single item.

This is not really hard, but it takes some practice. That is what we want to do in the laboratory.

| Review Questions | |

1. What is meant by a (direct) recursive method?
2. What is meant by a recursive definition? What are the two parts?
3. What is the value of 5! (5 factorial)?
4. What is returned by the method R given in the pre-lab reading if its parameter is "LAB"? In other words, what is the value of R("LAB")?

The Laboratory

| Objectives | |

- To become more comfortable with recursive methods.
- To write and test recursive methods.

| A Guide to the Laboratory | |

- Task 1 takes the example from the pre-lab reading of a sorting procedure and implements and tests it. Nothing is turned in.
- Task 2 shows how one can draw recursive patterns. This is primarily a demonstration. The post-laboratory section has an exercise that creates a recursive pattern using circles. Nothing is turned in.
- Tasks 3 and 4 require writing recursive functions. The gcd method will go in your Toolbox.java, while the sumofDigits method will be created and tested in a separate file. Turn in a copy of Toolbox.java (just the page containing gcd) and its test file GCDTest.java, plus a copy of SumDigitsTest.java.

Task 1: The Recursive Selection Sort—selectionSortRecursive

Add the `selectionSortRecursive` method described in the preliminary reading to your Toolbox class. Compile it. Then compile and run the program `SortDemo.java` that you can download for this lab. Run it several times with various values to see if the sort really does work.

We don't require a copy of `selectionSortRecursive` but you need to make sure it is correct as we will use it in a later laboratory.

Task 2: Recursive Patterns[1]

You can use recursion to create interesting geometric patterns. Download the two files `CanvasOfSquares.java` and `RecursiveSquares.java` and create a project containing these two files.

One file extends the Canvas class and modifies the `paint` method to draw a pattern of squares of decreasing sizes. It stops when the width of a square is smaller than some limiting value like 5. The other file has a simple `main` method that creates a CanvasOfSquares object and puts it in a ViewFrame object.

You will want to "Rebuild All" to compile both files and then run the program to see the pattern.

The key method is in `CanvasOfSquares` and is `drawSquares`. Read it carefully. Notice that it draws a square, reduces the width of the next squares to be drawn, and calls itself to put a square at its upper-left corner and a square at its upper-right corner. The first squares might look like the picture below. We

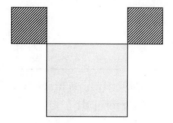

have added shading to emphasize the stages. (Actually, because of the way recursion works, the third square drawn by the program would not be the one on the upper right, but would be a smaller square drawn on the upper left of the upper-left shaded square! However, our picture gives you an idea of the pattern.)

Change one or more of the parameters in the `main` method when the canvas object is created. Then recompile and run it.

The methods `setInitialWidth`, `setReductionFactor`, and `setLimit` of `CanvasOfSquares` allow you to create an application that has such a canvas and can interact with the user and modify the various parameters for the drawing. We won't take the time to do that in this lab.

Task 3: GCD via Recursion

The greatest common divisor (gcd) of two integers, not both zero, is the largest number that can be factored out of both. It is always a positive value. For exam-

---

1. If you have not completed any exercises using methods of the Graphics class, you should read the lab "Drawing with Java."

ple, the gcd of 6 and 15 is 3. The gcd of -6 and 15 is also 3. The gcd of 12 and 0 is 12. 12 is the largest factor of 12 and 0 factors as 0*12, so 12 is a factor of 0.

Because the result is always positive, we will define the gcd of two integers assuming that they are not both 0 and that neither is negative. If values are negative, they will be replaced by their absolute values and then our definition will be applied.

We define `gcd(a,b)` as follows, assuming `a <= b`.

```
gcd(a,b) = b if a is 0
gcd(a,b) = gcd(b % a,a)
```

This is a recursive definition that produces the correct result. Let's trace `gcd(6,15)`.

```
gcd(6,15) = gcd(3,6) as 15 % 6 is 3
gcd(3,6) = gcd(0,3) as 6 % 3 is 0
gcd(0,3) is 3 by the first part of the definition.
```

Write the following method to add to the Toolbox class:

```
/**
 * Gives the greatest common divisor of the two
 * parameters, and assumes that both parameters cannot be
 * zero. One parameter can be zero and both or one could
 * be negative.
 */
public static int GCD(int a, int b)
{
    ...
}
```

Write a simple test program `GCDTest.java` that asks the user for two integers and displays the gcd value. The test program should not allow both integers to be 0. *Hint:* If a > b, you should just swap a and b and then apply the algorithm.

When it seems to be working, turn in a printout of your Toolbox.java file (just the page containing the GCD method) with your name on it. Also turn in a printout of your test program.

Task 4: The Sum of the Digits of an Integer via Recursion

In a file `SumDigitsTest.java`, write the method below and test it by calling it from `main`. Use a single file with a class `SumDigitsTest` containing the methods `main` and `sumDigits`. **Don't put the method in Toolbox.java.** Instead, create a simple `main` method to ask the user for an integer and call `sumDigits( )`.

```
// Returns the sum of the digits of the parameter n
// using recursion to do the sum.
public static int sumDigits(int n)
{
    ...
}
```

Hint: The easiest base case occurs when n is zero. It will also be easier if you replace any negative value of the parameter n by its absolute value. This avoids worrying about sign. Also, recall that if you focus on the right-most digit, it is not necessary to know how many digits there are in the number.

Key idea: The sum of the digits of a number n is the right-most digit n % 10 plus the sum of the digits of n / 10. n / 10 is the number n without its right-most digit.

Turn in a printout of your solution with your name(s) on it.

Post-Laboratory Exercises

Exercise 1

How could you modify the method `linearSearch` in your Toolbox so that it was done using recursion? Test the modification.

This is just an exercise. Recursion is probably not the natural way to approach a linear search.

Exercise 2

Look at the definition of the Fibonacci sequence in the preface to this laboratory. For the value F(6), how many times is F(3) computed? To answer this try to write out the individual steps of the computation.

You should quickly see that there is a lot of duplication of function calls in this recursion. This is a case where recursion is expensive. Try to count all the function calls for F(6).

Iteration or a simple loop can calculate the Fibonacci sequence much faster. Write both an iterative and recursive version of the following method:

```
// computes the n-th Fibonacci number, n >= 1
public static int fib(int n)
```

Exercise 3

What would happen if in the `CanvasOfSquares` class you had the `paint` method center the first square and `drawSquares` put smaller squares *at all four corners* rather than just the top corners? Make the modifications and test it.

Exercise 4

Using the file CanvasOfSquares.java as a model, create a class that extends Canvas called `CanvasOfCircles` and have the `paint` method find the center of the canvas. Then it should call a method called `drawCircles`, which will be given the center position and the radius along with a Graphics object g. It will draw that circle using `g.drawOval()` and then will call itself twice to draw other circles whose radii are the current radius multiplied by the reduction factor. These circles will have centers at the east and west positions of the first circle. Recall that `drawOval` expects the (x,y) position to be the upper-left corner of the enclosing rectangle.

Your reduction factor should be at most 0.5 for this problem. You should use `CanvasOfSquares` as a model, but you can omit the three methods that set the parameters. Replace `initialWidth` by `initialRadius`.

The test program should have main in the file `RecursiveCircles.java`. When you create the `CanvasOfCircles` object, use the values 100, 0.4, and 5 for its parameters.

Once the program is working, print out a copy of your `CanvasOfCircles.java` and `RecursiveCircles.java` files to turn in. Be sure your name is on each copy.

Exercise 5

Write the following method using paper and pencil. You must use recursion! Do this on a sheet of blank paper to turn in.

The method will reverse the items in the array cells A[first], A[first + 1], ..., A[last]. We assume that first <= last.

```
public static void ReverseArray(int[] A, int first, int last)
{
    . . .

}
```

You can write a small test program if you like, but that is not required.

Merge Sort—A Recursive Sort

This is just a preview of a recursive sorting algorithm that is more efficient than the selection sort algorithm.

MERGE

If you have two lists that are *individually sorted*, you probably already know how to merge them into a single list. This is really a simple idea. You examine the initial items on each list and move the smaller one to a new list. You continue to do this until one list is empty and then just move all of the items on the nonempty list to the new combined list. Call this operation MERGE. It results in a single sorted list.

Merge Sort Algorithm

The merge sort works as follows when given a list:
- If the list has one item or none, quit/return.
- Split the list into two halves and apply the merge sort to each half.
- Apply MERGE to the two sorted halves.

This is merge sort!

Test it by writing six or seven integers on small pieces of paper. Scramble them to form a random list. Carefully follow the steps of merge sort and use MERGE as described. This works and is very simple. Furthermore, we shall see that it is dramatically faster than the selection sort for large lists. This is not immediately obvious!

For now just try to understand how the algorithm works. We will code it in a later laboratory.

11

Linear Algorithms

By *linear algorithms* we mean the algorithms that are applied to linear collections:
- searching for an item in a list
- sorting a list

There are many naive algorithms to perform these tasks. We will want to find the *best* algorithms. By best we mean the algorithm that performs the task in the least time.[1] This seems like a simple idea but when comparing two algorithms, A and B, you may find that algorithm A is faster than B if the data size is small, but B is faster than A for large data sets. It may also be the case that there are some situations where the algorithm performs very poorly. For example, the quick sort algorithm is very fast (as its name implies) for randomly organized data, but for data lists that are sorted or nearly sorted, it runs very slowly. In practice, we use realistic data sets that are quite large. For example, a typical online dictionary may have 25,000 words. We also consider randomly organized data and sorted data when doing comparisons. The randomly organized data allows us to time the "average" case.

As an example, suppose we were using a computer-readable dictionary of words to create a spell-checking program. In this application, we must look up every word that occurs in a document in our dictionary, so *searching* for a word must be very fast. A linear search fails to take advantage of the ordering of the words in the dictionary. A binary search can be applied and is dramatically better than a linear search.

There are a number of *sorting* algorithms for general data. We have coded the selection sort in a previous laboratory using recursion. We will code an iterative version in this laboratory. In a later laboratory we will consider more efficient sorts.

We will code several algorithms and check them for correctness. The implementation will be in the form of methods that you will add to your Toolbox class.

---

1. In later courses you will encounter more formal measurements of the efficiency of algorithms that allow algorithms to be placed in simple categories. These formal measurements are proportional to our time measurements, so what we do here is quite reasonable for comparison purposes.

Pre-Laboratory Reading

Linear Search—A Quick Review

The linear search assumes nothing about the ordering of items in an array. In performing a search it starts with the first item and compares it with the special item being searched for. If there is a match it returns the position. Otherwise, it moves to the item in the next position and compares it with the special value. This continues until the item is found or the last element is examined. If the algorithm cannot find the value, then by convention it returns -1 to signal that the value was not found. Otherwise it returns the position where the item was first found.

If A is the array name, special is the item searched for, and first and last are the initial and final array positions to be examined, then the algorithm looks like this:

- Let P have the value of first.
- Repeat the following steps while P <= last:
    - If A[P] equals special, return P and exit the algorithm.
    - Increase P by 1.
- Return -1 as the value was not found.

This naturally codes as a for loop or a while loop. The for loop version looks like

```
for (int P = first; P <= last; P = P + 1)
{
    if (A[P] == special) // assuming primitive types
        return P;
}
return -1;
```

Your Toolbox class should already have the method linearSearch from the Collections laboratory. If not, be sure to add the method (int and double versions) before starting the laboratory.

The Binary Search Algorithm

The binary search is used to look for an item in a *sorted* list. It takes advantage of the fact that the list is ordered. It examines the middle item, and if the item is not found, the algorithm can eliminate half of the list based on whether the item searched for comes before or after the middle item. By eliminating half of the list after each examination, it does significantly fewer comparisons than the linear search.

Assume in the following algorithm that A is the name of the list and first, last, and middle refer to positions in the list. The value special will be the item that is being searched for on the list. The convention will be to produce/return the position where special is found or return -1 to indicate that it was not found.

Binary Search

- If last < first, cease the algorithm and return -1 as special cannot be found.
- Calculate middle to be (first + last) / 2 via integer division.
- If special is found at position middle of A, produce middle and cease.

- If `special` *comes before* the item at position `middle` of A, then restart the algorithm with `last` changed to `middle - 1`.
- If `special` *comes after* the item at position `middle` of A, then restart the algorithm with `first` changed to `middle + 1`.

A little thought shows that this could be coded using recursion or using a loop. If using a loop, the condition in the first step could be expressed in a method in the following form:

```
while(first <= last)
{
    ...
}
return -1; // not found
```

Checking Efficiency

We can do some simple checks to see how many comparisons it takes to find an item. We can consider the worst case—where `special` is not on the list A. The average case will take fewer comparisons.

Before doing so, note that if a list has n items and a linear search is used, then there must be n comparisons done to determine that an item is not on the list. On average, the linear search will have to examine half of the items on the list, or n/2 items. Can the binary search do better?

Consider the following array of items. Assume that we start with `first = 0` and `last = 19`. Complete the table for the values of `special`.

-12	0	2	9	11	22	23	30	33	34	35	48	51	56	58	74	79	80	85	88
0	1	2	3	4	5	6	7	8	9	10	11	12	13	14	15	16	17	18	19

Hint: Make a chart of the initial and changing values of `first`, `last`, and `middle`.

special	Value of `middle`	Number of Comparisons
5		
36		
57		

This list was fairly small. Let's consider a list of 1,000 items. Assume that we want a number that is *smaller* than any item on the list. (The same number of comparisons will be done. But the values of middle will be different if we use an arbitrary value not on the list.) The columns below show the values of `first`, `last`, and `middle`.

```
first   last    middle
-----   ----    ------
0       999     499
0       498     249
0       248     124
0       123     61
0       60      30
0       29      14
0       13      6
0       5       2
0       1       0
0       -1      STOP
```

We examined nine positions in the array—indicated by the values of middle. If we had started with 1,024 items, it would have taken 10 comparisons.

(Try it!) If we had used any number of items from 512 to 1,023, it would have taken nine comparisons to determine that the value was not on the list!

Interestingly, if we had 1,024 items and sought a value *larger* than any value on the list, it would take 11 comparisons. This can be checked by hand and compared with the similar check for seeking a number smaller than all items on the list.

This certainly takes fewer comparisons than a linear search. What is the pattern? The key is to note that the maximum number of comparisons changes at values like 256; 512; 1,024; 2,048; and so on (i.e., powers of 2). This makes sense when you realize that the list is being halved at each comparison.

```
512  = 2^9
1024 = 2^10
```

The logarithm to base 2 of a number is just the exponent when the number is expressed as 2 to a power. We will write `log2()` for this function and note that log2(512) is 9 and log2(1,024) is 10. log2(1,000) is between 9 and 10 and is a floating point value.

We can summarize the preceding discussion by saying:

> If a binary search is used to examine a list of n items for an item not on the list, then the maximum number of comparisons is the floor of `log2(n)+1`.

Recall that the *floor* of a number like 9.8 is 9.0, while the floor of 10.0 is 10.0.

We now can have a chart of the *worst* case for a binary and a linear search for some large values.

Size of List	Linear Search—Maximum Comparisons	Binary Search—Maximum Comparisons
1,024	1,024	11
2,048	2,048	12
4,096	4,096	13
1,000,000	1,000,000	20
1,000,000,000	1,000,000,000	30

If your dictionary has 25,000 words, what is the maximum number of comparisons that will be done to look up a word if you use a binary search?

Selection Sort Recalled

The code for a recursive version of the selection sort was given in the laboratory on recursive methods. You were asked to add the method below

```
public static void selectionSortRecursive(int[] A, int first, int last)
{
    if (first >= last)
    {
        return; // at most one item
    }
    int p = maxOnList(A, first, last);
    swap(A, p, last);
    selectionSortRecursive(A, first, last - 1);
}
```

to your Toolbox class.

An *iterative* version (note the name change) would look like

```
public static void selectionSortIterative(int[] A, int first, int last)
{
    while (first < last)   // two items at least
    {
        int p = positionOfMax(A, first, last);
        swap(A, p, last);
        last = last - 1;
    }
}
```

We could have used the condition `first <= last`, but with only one item, the largest is already in the last position!

You will find that the iterative version is slightly more efficient and will want to use it instead of the recursive version.

In the laboratory we will add this method to the Toolbox class.

Efficiency of Selection Sort

We note that the `positionOfMax` method must examine every item in the part of the list it is passed. We can easily count the number of comparisons and swaps used to sort an array of N items.

- The inside of the loop is done N - 1 times, so there are N - 1 swaps.
- The lists given to `positionOfMax` have sizes N, then N - 1, then N - 2, . . ., then 2, so the number of comparisons is (N - 1) + (N - 2) + . . . + 3 + 2 + 1.

From discrete mathematics it is possible to show that the last sum is

```
N * (N - 1) / 2
```

Algebra can be used to show that the total number of comparisons and swaps is

```
N * (N - 1) / 2 + N - 1 = (N * N) / 2 + N / 2 - 1
```

As N gets large, the first term, N * N / 2, dominates. For that reason we say the selection sort is an *"N-squared" algorithm*. The time taken to sort large arrays containing N items will be approximately proportional to N squared.

Review Questions

1. If an array has N items, how many items must be examined to determine that a special item is not in the array if the linear search algorithm is used?

2. What must be true of an array in order to use the binary search algorithm?

3. If an array has N items, how many items must be examined to determine that a special item is not in the array if the binary search algorithm is used?

4. Why do we say that the selection sort is an N-squared algorithm?

The Laboratory

Objectives

- To implement and test the binary search algorithm.
- To create a simple method to test to see if an array is sorted or not.

A Guide to the Laboratory

We will be writing and testing the following methods:
- binarySearch
- selectionSortIterative
- isSorted

All the methods will be added to Toolbox.java. You will be writing two versions for each—one for int data and the other for double data.

Task 1: Coding and Testing a Binary Search

Add the following method to your toolbox:

```
public static int binarySearch(int[] A, int first,
                               int last, int Special)
```

It can be written iteratively or recursively—your choice.

Now create a project containing three files—`BinaryTest.java`, `BinarySearchTester.java`, and `Toolbox.java`. The first two files may be downloaded and added to the project.

The BinaryTest class (shown below) creates a sorted array of a small size, say at most 20 to 25 items, and then creates an instance of a class called `BinarySearchTester`.

```
// BinaryTest.java
// Creates a testing object for the method Toolbox.binarySearch
// using a sorted array of integers.

public class BinaryTest
{
    public static void main(String[] args)
    {
        int[] A = {-5, -2, 0, 8, 12, 13, 16, 22, 25, 27, 30, 31, 32, 33,
                36, 42, 47, 50, 55, 65, 98};
        new BinarySearchTester(A);
    }
}
```

The BinarySearchTester class will take the array sent to it via its constructor and display the items in a ViewFrame output area so the tester knows what is in the array. It will also have a button that will allow the user to enter an item to search for. The object will display one of the messages "Found at position. . ." or "Not found" in the output area.

A sample window for the BinarySearchTester object might look like the one below after an initial look for an item. We have set IOEcho to be true and used a ViewFrame object. The array should be a data field of the class BinarySearchTest, as should the ViewFrame object. The action class for the button should be an inner class of BinarySearchTest and have access to the array and the ViewFrame object.

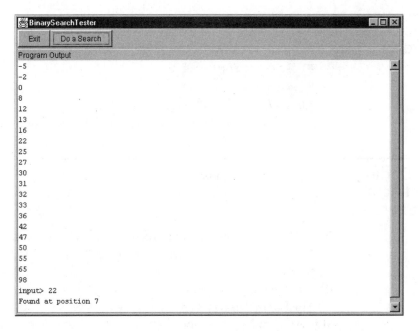

You are to test the method `binarySearch` by compiling and running the project and doing searches for items in or not in the array. Modify the array created in BinaryTest.java so that it has an even number of items and compile and test some more.

Once the `binarySearch` method seems to be working correctly for integers, enter a version for the type `double` in your Toolbox class.

```
public static int binarySearch(double[] A, int first, int last, double Special)
```

Modify the files BinaryTest.java and BinarySearchTester.java to properly test this version.

Task 2: Writing and Testing the isSorted Method

We will want to test the code to sort arrays. We need to quickly know whether or not an array is sorted. Add the following methods to your Toolbox class. All return true if the array A is sorted and false otherwise. We assume that `first<=last` where `first` is the initial position of the array and `last` is the final position. We may have situations where we only want to look at part of an array. That is why we use `first` and `last`.

```
public static boolean isSorted(int[] A, int first, int last)
public static boolean isSorted(double[] A, int first, int last)
```

Be sure to document the methods in JavaDoc style and test them with a simple test program. The arrays used to test can be small (four to five items).

The algorithm to determine if something is sorted is very simple. You should be able to come up with the idea. (*Hint:* Just think about how you would decide if a printed list that you were reading through was not in order.)

Task 3: Testing selectionSort Iterative

Create a project containing `Toolbox.java` and a test file called `SelectionTest.java`. The latter file will have a simple `main` method that creates an array of values, calls `selectionSortIterative`, then prints "OK" or "Problem" depending upon the result of calling `isSorted` to check the result.

The iterative version of selection sort is given in the pre-lab reading. Enter it in your Toolbox class. You may want to use a ViewFrame for input and output and ask the user how big the array should be and what the values should be. Just be sure it is sufficient to reasonably test the `selectionSortIterative` method.

Turn in a printout of your Toolbox.java file with the methods binarySearch, selectionSortIterative, and isSorted clearly marked. Also turn in copies of your test programs for tasks 2 and 3.

Post-Laboratory Exercises

Once your binary search method is working properly, convert it to work with arrays of String objects so it could be used in a dictionary search.

```
public static int binarySearch(String[] A, int first, int last, String Special)
```

Make the minor changes to BinaryTest.java and BinearySearchTest.java to be sure they properly test the method.

Did you remember to use `compareTo()` instead of < or ==?

LABORATORY *12*

Sorting Out Sorts

A binary search depends on having a sorted array. If a large number of searches are to be done, then it is efficient to sort the array and use the binary search. If only one or two lookups are to be done, then a linear search is more efficient as we omit the time required to sort the array.

How much time does it take to sort an array of size N? The answer depends on the sorting algorithm used. In this laboratory we will examine a new sort called the *merge sort* and compare it with the *selection sort* that was introduced in an earlier laboratory. Our comparison will be based on timings of the algorithms coded in Java. We will explore Java's mechanism for keeping time and discuss problems in collecting timing data.

The post-laboratory section will introduce a third algorithm called *quick sort* and discuss its implementation and efficiency.

Pre-Laboratory Reading

The Merge Sort Algorithm	From the laboratory on recursive methods, we recall the basic description of the merge sort algorithm. Assume that if you have two lists that are *individually sorted*, you know how to merge them into a single sorted list. You examine the initial items on each list and move the smaller one to a new list, then advance to the next item of the list where the smaller value was found. You continue to do this until one list is empty and then just move all of the items on the non-empty list to the new combined list. This operation is called MERGE.

The *merge sort* works as follows when given a list:
- If the list has one item or no items, quit/return.
- Split the list into two halves and apply merge sort to each half.
- Apply MERGE to the two sorted halves.

Let us now be more formal in the statement of the algorithm; in particular, we need to be more explicit in describing the MERGE algorithm.

MERGE

Let A and B be sorted lists. Assume that the first and last positions of A are first_A and last_A. Assume that the first and last positions of B are first_B and last_B. Assume that first_A <= last_A and first_B <= last_B.

Let M be an array of size large enough to hold all of the elements of A and B that are to be merged. Its initial index will be first_M. The array M will be the merger of the other two arrays.

Use three integer variables a, b, and m refer to positions in A, B, and M, respectively. Their initial values are first_A, first_B, and first_M, respectively.

Repeat the following step until either a > last_A or b > last_B, which indicates that the list A or the list B, respectively, is emptied.
- If A[a] comes before B[b], then set M[m] to A[a] and increase both m and a by 1. Otherwise set M[m] to B[b] and increase both m and b by 1.

To complete the algorithm, determine which list is not yet empty and copy all of its remaining elements to the end of M.

When MERGE is coded as a procedure, it will have eight parameters: A, first_A, last_A, B, first_B, last_B, M, and first_M. The array M will have any existing values overwritten during the algorithm, while A and B will have no changes in their elements.

Merge Sort

Once MERGE is written we can describe merge sort precisely.

Assume we have an array T with initial position first_T and final position last_T. We wish to sort T[first_T], . . ., T[last_T].
- If last_T <= first_T, quit/return as there is at most one item.
- Let middle be (first_T + last_T) / 2, calculated using integer division.
- Apply merge sort to T from positions first_T to middle.
- Apply merge sort to T from positions middle + 1 to last_T.
- Create an array temp that has last_T - first_T + 1 cells.
- Apply MERGE to the two (now sorted) halves of T using temp as the array where the merged halves are placed.

- Copy the contents of temp to T from first_T to last_T. In temp the initial position is 0.

The last two steps must be separate. We cannot merge the two halves of T directly into T, as we would overwrite some values. This is why we use an array M in the algorithm for MERGE. The array temp above would be passed as a parameter that corresponds to M when the MERGE procedure is called.

Efficiency

The efficiency of merge sort is not obvious because of the recursion. The total number of comparisons in MERGE is at most the sum of the number of items in the arrays A and B. This is because an item gets moved to M after each comparison.

If the number of items in T is a power of 2, then it is not hard to show via algebra that the number of comparisons and copies is proportional to N * Log2(N) where N is the number of items in T. (We omit the algebra and save the analysis for a later course.) Compare this with the time proportional to N * N = N^2 for the selection sort.

Generating Random Data for Tests

We will want to test the coding of sort algorithms on large sets of random data. We also will want to compare the time it takes to sort large arrays of random values using each coded algorithm.

We can generate such arrays using Java's Random class, which is in the package java.util. The code below shows how this might be done using the nextDouble() method, which returns a pseudorandom[1] value between 0.0 and 1.0.

```
double[] d = new double[4096];
Random r = new Random();
for (int i = 0; i < 4096; i++)
   d[i] = r.nextDouble();
```

The code will fill the array d with 4,096 random values, each in the range 0.0 to 1.0.

Timing

Java has a way to represent the current time by creating a Date object with the information about the current moment. Date is one of the classes in the java.util package. The Date object is initialized with the number of milliseconds since January 1, 1970. This is a very large integer and is stored as a long type value. The method getTime() of the Date class returns this long value. The code below shows how a simple timing might be done. Notice that we create a Date object and then immediately call its getTime method—we don't even name the Date object.

```
// DateTimeTest.java
// just tests Date object's use for measuring time

import LabPkg.*;
```

---

1. The term "pseudorandom" is used because such values are not truly random in the mathematical sense. Each value is generated from the previous value using an algorithm that attempts to make any value between 0.0 and 1.0 have the same probability of being generated. The first value's calculation is based on a user-provided value called a "seed" or is based on the current time.

```
import java.util.*;

public class DateTimeTest
{
    public static void main(String[] args)
    {
        ViewFrame vf = new ViewFrame();
        vf.setVisible(true);

        long timeStart = new Date().getTime();  // initial time
        Useful.pause(56);                        // event being timed
        long timeStop = new Date().getTime();    // stopping time
        vf.println("Start at " + timeStart);
        vf.println("Stop at " + timeStop);
        vf.println("Duration (seconds): "
        + Toolbox.roundDouble((timeStop - timeStart) / 1000.0,2));
    }
}
```

We really only care about *elapsed time,* which is the final value printed. We divide by 1000.0 to convert the milliseconds to seconds as a double, but we round the result to two decimal places using one of our Toolbox utility methods. The `Useful.pause(56)` should cause a delay of 5.6 seconds. The result of a run is shown below.

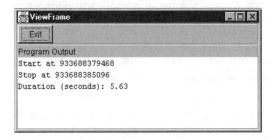

Notice that the result is not 5.60. This is due to the small amount of time its takes to do the creation of the second Date object. If this program is run several times there will be some small differences in that second decimal place due to system overhead during object creation and the crudeness of Java's time-keeping. If the event being timed is of short duration, then the inaccuracy in the measurement can be quite large as a fraction of the elapsed time.

Review Questions

1. What method of the Random class is used to get a random value between 0.0 and 1.0?

2. What Java class can be used to get information about the current time?

3. If sorted arrays X and Y have 20 and 15 items respectively, what is the maximum number of comparisons done by a MERGE of X and Y?

4. If an array A has 1,024 items, the time to sort it using merge sort is proportional to what value?

The Laboratory

A Guide to the Laboratory

■ Tasks 1 and 2 demonstrate the generation of random data for testing and the vagaries of timing using Java's Date class.

- Tasks 3 and 4 require you to write and test the methods MERGE and mergeSort. The methods are placed in your Toolbox class.
- Task 5 uses a provided program to collect timing data for sorting large arrays using selection sort and merge sort. You are asked to draw conclusions from the analysis of the data.

Task 1: Generating Random Data

Write a simple program called RandomGeneration.java that will request N, the number of values desired, and then generate a list of N random double values. Use a ViewFrame for input and output.

Turn in a printout of the program.

Task 2: Timing Variability

Download the file DateTimeTest.java and modify it to ask the user to enter the pause amount (rather than use 56). Be sure that the code asking for the pause amount is not part of what is being timed! You can solve this problem by putting the code to request the pause amount immediately before the declaration of the variable timeStart.

- Run the program four times with the pause value of 10 (1 second) and record the average duration time.
- Run the program four times with the pause value of 100 (10 seconds) and record the average duration time.
- Run the program four times with the pause value of 200 (20 seconds) and record the average duration time.

What conclusions do the data suggest concerning the accuracy of timing using this method? Write this up to turn in along with the data you collected.

Task 3: Writing and Testing MERGE

For each of the methods MERGE and mergeSort that you are to write, you should do versions for integer and double arrays. We will not need a String version for this laboratory.

Add the method below to your Toolbox class following the algorithm in the pre-laboratory reading.

```
public static void MERGE(int[] A, int first_A, int last_A,
                int[]B, int first_B, int last_B,
                int[] M, first_M)
```

Be sure to add the comments.

Write a test program that will create two sorted arrays and call MERGE. Display the resulting merged array in a ViewFrame output window. The two sorted arrays might be "manually" created via a declaration like

```
int[] T = {20, 30, 34, 35, 56,70};
int[] S = {1, 2, 3, 25, 36};
```

The array to hold the merged values of T and S would be declared as

```
int[] Ans = new int[T.length + S.length];
```

Don't forget to do a version where the parameters A and B are arrays of type double and the method fills an array of type double. It is also useful to have a version for arrays of String objects but that is optional at this time.

| Task 4: Coding and Testing Merge Sort | Using the algorithm in the pre-laboratory reading, add the following methods to your Toolbox class: |

```
public static void mergeSort(int[] A, int first, int last)
public static void mergeSort(double[] A, int first, int last)
```

You can write a simple test program to create an array of random data values, call `mergeSort`, and then use `isSorted` to see if it worked properly. The input might be the number of items to be sorted and the output could be a simple message indicating "Success" or a "Problem."

Create a printout of your test program to turn in. Turn in a printout of the pages of `Toolbox.java` containing the `MERGE` and `mergeSort` methods. Be sure your name is on the pages.

| Task 5: Finding the Better Sort | We want to make three claims and see if we can collect empirical evidence to support them. |

- **Claim #1:** For reasonably large values of N, the array size, the time it takes selection sort to sort the entire array is proportional to N*N for random data.
- **Claim #2:** For reasonably large values of N, the array size, the time it takes merge sort to sort the entire array is proportional to N*log2(N) for random data.
- **Claim #3:** Merge sort is significantly faster than selection sort, and the improvement increases with N.

We now want to run selection sort and merge sort on large random data sets and record their running time. The sizes of the data sets must be at least 4,000, because for smaller size arrays the time for the sorts cannot be measured precisely enough to reliably detect the real time differences. Since we claimed that the time for merge sort is proportional to N*Log2(N), it is useful to use powers of 2 for the values of N.

The following values should be used for array sizes in the tests:

```
4096
8192
16384
32768
65536
```

You will create a project containing two files—`SortTester.java` and `SortTest.java` (both files are available for downloading)—plus your Toolbox.java file.

The file SortTest.java will have a short `main` method that will create two instances of SortTester, one that will use the selection sort and one that will use the merge sort. Each will have an action button labeled "Time a sort" that will pop up a request for the array size to be used, then request how many arrays to sort, and finally create the arrays of that size and fill them with random values. Then it will time how long the sort operations take for all of those arrays. The output will show the average time for each of the arrays to be sorted. The SortTester object will have a ViewFrame object, and the title of the ViewFrame object will be the name of the sort being tested. The output area of the ViewFrame object will contain the results of the test. Be sure that `setIOEcho(true)` is called so you can be sure you record the array size properly. Examples of the two SortTester objects are shown below.

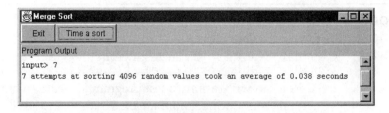

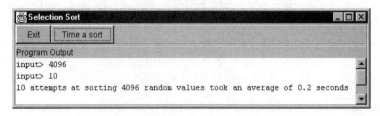

You should have the following static data values of the class SortTester, which are used with the constructor to signal which sort is to be used.

```
public static final int SELECTIONSORT = 1;
public static final int MERGESORT = 2;
public static final int QUICKSORT =3;
```

The last one will be used when we test another useful sort later.

Once you have compiled the project, run it and time each sort using the sizes specified in the table below and record the results. The program displays the time in seconds to at most three decimal places. The program allows you to specify how many sortings will be timed (up to 10 in any single run) and produces the average sorting time. This is designed to reduce the role of overhead in creating the timing objects.

N	Log2(N)	Selection Sort Time	Merge Sort Time
4096	12	(5)	(5)
8192	13	(4)	(5)
16384	14	(3)	(5)
32768	14	(2)	(5)
65536	15	(1)	(5)

The number of sorts per run is indicated in parentheses in the table. Fill in the average time per run. *Warning:* You will find that the selection sort may take a *very* long time to do the 65536 size array sort.

Please note that because Java does not measure time as accurately as desired and because the time can be affected by other programs running on the computer you will get "noise" in your data. Do the best you can to answer the questions below.

1. What conclusions can you draw from this comparison?

2. Which claims are supported?

3. Does it appear that the selection sort's time is proportional to N*N?

4. Does it appear that the merge sort's time is proportional to N*Log2(N)?

Write up your data and your conclusions for submission. Be sure to use proper grammar. Be neat.

Post-Laboratory Reading

Quick Sort

Quick sort, or quicksort, is another recursive sort that has a running time proportional to N * Log2(N) where N is the number of items. For random data it is faster than merge sort because it has a smaller constant of proportionality. However, if the data is already nearly in order, the usual algorithm can be very slow, like the selection sort.

There are clever ways to code quick sort and you will explore them in another course or you can find details in your textbook. We simply give the algorithm, where as usual A will be an array to be sorted from position `first` to position `last`.

- If `last <= first`, then quit/return as there is at most one item.
- Select one element of the array and call it the "pivot."
- Shuffle the elements of the array so that all the elements that are less than or equal to the pivot element (including the pivot element itself) are at the beginning of the array and all the elements greater than the pivot are at the end of the array. Let P be the position where the elements larger than the pivot start. Hence, all the elements A[first],...,A[P - 1] are less than or equal to the pivot and all elements A[P],...,A[last] are larger than the pivot. By doing a swap, make sure that the original pivot value is in A[P - 1].
- Call quick sort on A from `first` to P - 2.
- Call quick sort on A from P to `last`.

The "shuffle" step guarantees that the selected pivot element is put in its proper place in the sorted array, i.e., the place where it will end up when the whole array is sorted. One coding approach that works is to create a temporary array of the appropriate size, and copy items from A to it so that the shuffle step is accomplished. Then copy the shuffled items back to A. (The best implementation of the algorithm is able to do the shuffle step without a temporary array.)

If the data is random and the pivot is a random element, then the position P will be approximately in the middle from first to last with high probability. Hence the recursive calls are dealing with arrays that are only half as large. Of course, this is a probabilistic statement, and it is rare that an array splits exactly in half.

Quick sort gets into trouble and is slow if the pivot element is the largest or smallest item of the array. Then one recursive call has an empty array while the other has the entire array except for the pivot element. Hence, it looks like the recursive version of selection sort in terms of time.

Analysis of quick sort is difficult because of the dependence on the value of the pivot. Experimentation can convince you that it is superior to merge sort for random data.

Exercise

Add a method `quickSort` to `Toolbox.java` following the algorithm above. Test it for correctness using random data and the `isSorted` method. Then use `SortTester.java` and a modified `SortTest.java` to collect timing data. Is it faster than merge sort on random data?

13

I/O and Exceptions

We have used pop-up dialog boxes for input and have written to text areas, but we have managed to avoid two areas of *input/output (I/O)* that now need our attention:

- reading from and writing to files on a disk
- input from the keyboard in a command line environment such as a terminal window—called console input

Fewer and fewer applications use console I/O as graphical user interfaces dominate our computer environments. But many applications work with files. For that reason we will focus on file reading and writing. Console I/O will be explained with a simple example, but it will not be central to the laboratory.

Exceptions must be understood in order to perform I/O in Java. They are useful in other contexts as well. Generically, an *exception* is a signal that something special and unusual has occurred. How the signal is made known to the running program and how the programmer develops the code for an appropriate response is called the *exception handling mechanism*. Java's mechanism is fairly simple. The only reason it was not introduced earlier is because it requires an additional language structure—the "try-catch" clause—and we didn't want to overwhelm you early in the course. In this lab we will explain and use Java's exception handling mechanism in simple examples.

Pre-Laboratory Reading

We have organized the reading into four sections:
- Exceptions
- File Input
- File Output
- Console I/O

Exceptions

Basic Facts

- Exceptions are *objects* that carry information about an abnormal event.
- Exceptions are created and "thrown" by methods. They are passed back along the sequence of method calls until "caught."
- An "uncaught" exception normally results in abnormal termination of a nongraphics program. Programs with graphical objects such as windows continue in the sense that the graphical objects persist and the Java interpreter continues to run. The Java interpreter reports the exception on the error output stream.

What are these abnormal events? Typical examples are
- division by 0
- the referencing of an array location with an invalid index

```
int[] A = {4, 9, 12};
int y = A[7];    // the array only has three cells!
```

- invalid data—for example, the method `Integer.parseInt()` expects a string parameter like "253" and produces the integer 253, but throws an exception if given the string "hello"

An Example

A common mistake is having a reference that is to be initialized in a constructor, but in the constructor declaring the reference again as a local variable. Consider the following code and see that the ViewFrame reference vf is declared twice. The two places are in bold. The first declaration has the default initial value of null. In the method `showSecret`, the statement `vf.println(...);` has a `vf` that refers to the one initialized to null and throws the NullPointerException.

```
// SecretValue.java
import LabPkg.*;
public class SecretValue
{
    ViewFrame vf;    // used for I/O
    int secret;      // the secret number

    // parameter n will be the initial secret number
    public SecretValue(int n)
    {
        secret = n;
        ViewFrame vf = new ViewFrame("SecretValue Window");
        vf.setVisible(true);
    }

    public void showSecret()
    {
        vf.println("Secret = " + secret); // exception occurs here
    }
```

```
// we put a simple main here to create a SecretValue object
 public static void main(String[] args)
{
    SecretValue x = new SecretValue(25);
    x.showSecret();
}
}
```

When the program runs, the following appears in the output window:

java.lang.NullPointerException

    at SecretValue.showSecret(SecretValue.java:23)

    at SecretValue.main(SecretValue.java:32)

Notice that the output says the problem occurs on line 23 and in the method showSecret. (If your file gets "double-spaced" during download the line number values will be different.)

You can download, compile, and run this program. To fix it, look in the constructor and replace

ViewFrame vf = new ...

with

vf = new ...

i.e., get rid of the ViewFrame adjective, which makes this vf a local variable in the constructor.

Declaration Rule

If a method will *possibly* throw an exception, the method must indicate this as shown in the example below

```
public void DoSomething() throws FunkyException
{
    // code for function
}
```

But...

Any exception that is an extension of the class RuntimeException is not required to be declared as possibly being thrown by the method. Examples are

- ArithmeticException
- ArrayIndexOutOfBoundsException
- NullPointerException

The Java Virtual Machine (the interpreter) catches these run-time exceptions and displays a stack trace. For nongraphics applications this usually terminates the program, as the main method is finished. Graphics applications are not terminated but may not behave properly.

I/O Exceptions

The extensions to the RuntimeException class need not be mentioned by the programmer, but all other exceptions must be mentioned in a method's definition. The most common types of exceptions occur during input and output operations. In the package java.io we find the following exceptions (in the online documentation for a package like java.io, the exceptions are listed after all the other classes):

- IOException—thrown by most input/output operations
- EOFException—an indication that a read past the end of the file was attempted
- FileNotFoundException—obvious

The class BufferedReader is found in java.io and is used to efficiently read in a file. It has a method readLine with the declaration

```
public String readLine() throws IOException
```

This means that when we use `readLine` to access a file we could have an exception occur. We may want to examine the exception and continue on with the program. This is called "catching" the exception.

Thread.sleep Method

In the class Thread a static method `sleep` is defined. Its parameter gives the number of milliseconds to pause before execution. It is declared with the phrase "throws InterruptedException." In this case when the pause is over the exception is thrown and acts like an alarm clock signal. This is the key to implementation of the method `pause` in the class `Useful` in the package `LabPkg`.

Try/Catch Rule

Any time you *call* a function that throws an exception (that is not an extension of RuntimeException), you must use a `try-catch` clause as show below:

```
try
{
    DoSomething();  // could throw an exception
    // other statements that could throw exceptions are possible
}
catch (FunkyException e)
{
    //... some action
}
```

The body of the catch part of the try-catch is where you can examine the exception and take action.

The `Thread.sleep` method is used as follows to pause the program for five seconds:

```
try {Thread.sleep(5000);} catch(InterruptedException e){}
```

In this case the catch part really has nothing to do so it is just a pair of curly braces.

What happens when an exception occurs within a try block that contains many statements? The quick answer is that the statements *after* the statement that generated the exception are skipped and the catch part is examined to see if the parameter is of the type of the exception. If the exception is of the type specified in the catch part's parameter, then the code in the catch part's block is executed. Then the next code to be executed is *after* the try-catch clause; the remaining statements in the try block are skipped.

Multiple Catch Clauses

There may be two or more types of exceptions that could occur in a try block and you want to handle each differently. It is possible to have several catch clauses associated with a single try clause. In the following code fragment, suppose that the statements in the try block could potentially generate an *EvilException* and a *NotSoBadException,* both of which extend the Exception class.

```
try
{
    ... statements
}
catch(EvilException ee)
{
    ... action for a bad event, probably kill the program
}
catch(NotSoBadException ne)
{
    ... action for benign exception
}
```

This is not needed in most of our situations involving I/O operations.

Throwing an Exception

You can write code that will generate an exception when your code is trying to detect an abnormal event. The code generates the exception with a *throws clause*. A trivial example is

```
if (something abnormal happens)
{
    throw new Exception("Bad things occurred in ...");
}
```

In this example we created a generic Exception object with the given message. We could have written a special extension of the Exception class and thrown an instance of it.

Summary

If you use a method that throws an exception, the call must be inside a try-catch. (However, if the exception is one that extends RuntimeException, the try-catch is optional.)

If you write a method that could possibly throw an exception, then you must indicate that the method throws the exception in the header line for the method. (Once again, you may ignore this requirement if the exception is one that extends RuntimeException.)

If you explicitly wish to generate an exception, then use a throw statement of the form

```
throw exception_object;
```

We will provide more examples during the laboratory. There are other things we could say about exceptions, but this covers the basics needed for this laboratory.

File Input

Files are named collections of data that reside on a computer's disk drives. Files could be executable programs like Netscape.exe, readable files like Toolbox.java, or data files in special formats.

A text file is one that consists of characters that can be printed and read by a human without special processing. Files like those created in Microsoft Word are readable on the screen but are not text files because they contain special unreadable-by-humans characters that provide formatting information such as boldface, font type, and so on. In practice, text files are line-oriented and may be read or written a line at a time or a character at a time. The newline character '\n' is used to mark the end of lines. Text files will be the focus of our attention in this laboratory.

Java provides a number of classes that assist in reading files. We shall examine two classes that are simple to use: `FileReader` and `BufferedReader`. FileReader is a class that encapsulates the mechanism to access a file on a disk. It "opens" the file for reading by making appropriate requests of the computer's operating system. It can be used to access the file's contents but only in a somewhat inefficient way.

The `BufferedReader` class provides an easier way to access file information. It hides some of the details of how reading a file works. It also provides some efficiency by reading a large chunk of the file into memory and then having the methods `readLine` and `read` access the memory rather than the disk.

The `readLine` method reads all the characters up to a newline and returns them as a string. If there are no more lines, the method returns `null`. The `read` method reads a character but returns it as an integer[1]. If end-of-file is reached, it returns -1.

The following line creates a FileReader object and passes it to the constructor of a BufferedReader.

```
BufferedReader fileIn = new BufferedReader(new FileReader(filename));
```

The constructor for FileReader can throw a FileNotFoundException and the methods `readLine` and `read` of BufferedReader can throw IOExceptions. For that reason these operations must be part of a try-catch clause.

Line-Oriented Example

Consider the following program, which requests a file name from a user, opens the file, then reads each line of the file, and displays each line with line numbers in the output area. We have used boldface to highlight some special features. (The file is available for downloading.)

```
// File: FileView.java
// Description: Program to display a file with line numbers prepended to each
//              line. Shows use of exceptions. Reads file name from a
//              pop-up dialog.

import java.io.*;
import LabPkg.*;

public class FileView
{
    public static void main(String[] args)
    {
        ViewFrame vf = new ViewFrame("FileView");
          vf.setVisible(true);
        String filename = vf.readString("Enter the file name");
        filename = filename.trim();
          // declare these outside the try block but use them in the try
        BufferedReader fileIn = null;
        int lineNumber = 0;
        String line;
        try
        {
            fileIn = new BufferedReader(new FileReader (filename) );
            line = fileIn.readLine();
            while (line != null)
            {
                lineNumber++;
                vf.println(lineNumber + "   " + line);
                line = fileIn.readLine();
            }
        }
        catch(Exception e) // catches FileNotFoundException and IOException
        {
            System.out.println(e);
        }
        // close the stream
        if (fileIn != null)
        {
            try {fileIn.close();} catch (Exception e) { }
        }

    }

} // end of class
```

We note the key lines in the order they appear within the program.

---

1. This seems strange, but internally, a char value is stored as a small, non-negative integer. So this is not inconsistent.

```
import java.io.*;
```
This import line is required for all I/O in Java and gives access to key classes and exceptions.

The lines

BufferedReader fileIn = null;

and

fileIn = new BufferedReader(new FileReader (filename));

were mentioned in the initial discussion. The variable `fileIn` is of type `BufferedReader`. If the file does not exist or cannot be opened for some reason, an exception is thrown by the FileReader constructor and the variable fileIn is never changed from its initial null value. The catch clause causes the message associated with the exception to be printed and then the code after the catch is executed. More could be done in the catch block if desired.

The other key line that performs most of the work is

```
line = fileIn.readLine();
```

Here, we call on the `readLine` method of `fileIn` to get the next line from the file and assign it to the String variable `line`. The value assigned to `line` is then compared with the value `null` in the condition of the while loop. If there is a line to read, the value of `line` will not be `null`. If we have reached the end of the file and it is not possible to read another line, then `readLine` returns `null`. We have adopted the strategy here of doing a "priming read" before we enter the loop so that we have a meaningful value in `line` when we first encounter the condition of the while loop. The second call to the `readLine` method at the end of the loop reads a new line from the file each time the loop is executed. Without this call, we would have an infinite loop.

After reading all information from a file, the file should be "closed." Normally when the program terminates all files are closed, but there are cases where a file might be read several times. Then it must be closed and reopened. We explicitly close the file to show how it is done. The statement

```
try {fileIn.close();} catch(Exception e) {}
```

closes the file. The `close` method throws an IOException so the try-catch is required. It is highly unlikely that a file cannot be closed, so we didn't put anything inside the catch block.

Token-Oriented Example

Often we need to read data such as numbers from a file. If the file is a text file, there may be any number of values on each line. The technique used to obtain the data is

- read entire lines one at a time into a String variable using the method readLine,
- for each line read, create a StringTokenizer object with tokens that will be the data you want to read.

The program below illustrates how this can work on a file containing integer values. The files `FileSum.java` and `IntData.txt` may be downloaded. The latter is a simple text file containing integers.

```
// File: FileSum.java
// Programmer:
// Description: Reads in integer data from a text file. The values are
//              summed and the total displayed.

import java.io.*;
import java.util.*;  // for StringTokenizer
```

```
import LabPkg.*;

public class FileSum
{
 public static void main(String[] args)
 {

  ViewFrame vf = new ViewFrame("FileSum");
  vf.setIOEcho(true);
  vf.setVisible(true);
  String fname = vf.readString("Enter a file name for the data");
  fname = fname.trim();
  BufferedReader in = null;
  // try to open the file
  try
  {
      in = new BufferedReader(new FileReader(fname));
  }
  catch (Exception e)
  {
      vf.println("Unable to open file " + fname);
      vf.println("" + e);
      System.exit(0);
  }

  StringTokenizer st;
  String line = null;
  int total = 0;
  try
  {
      // read lines until end of file
      while ((line = in.readLine()) != null) // readLine throws exceptions
      {
              st = new StringTokenizer(line);
              if (st.countTokens() == 0) continue; // empty line
              while (st.hasMoreTokens())
              {
                      int current = Integer.parseInt(st.nextToken());
                      total += current;
                      vf.println("Read in " + current);
              }
      }
  }
  catch (Exception e)
  {
      System.out.println( e );
      e.printStackTrace();      // sometimes useful
      System.exit(0);           // terminates the program
  }
   // no errors
   vf.println("Total is " + total);
 }

} // end of class
```

Notice that we use two try-catch clauses. The first is just to check to see if the file can be opened. If the open fails, we terminate the program with `System.exit(0)`.

The remaining code reads lines from the file with `readLine`. Notice that we have chosen a different strategy for our input loop in this program. The line

```
while ((line = in.readLine()) != null)
```

does double duty here, taking advantage of the fact that in Java, all expressions have a value, including an assignment expression. The condition of the while loop contains the call to the `readLine` method and the resulting assignment to the variable `line`. This assignment statement is enclosed in parentheses (these are necessary in this context!) indicating that we are using the "value" of the assignment expression in the comparison of the while loop. The value of an assignment statement is the value that is assigned to the variable on the left-hand side of the assignment operator. It is this value that is compared to `null` in the loop condition. This organization is more compact than the loop with a priming read that we used earlier, and it has exactly the same behavior. In your own programs, you should use whichever version of the file input loop you feel most comfortable with.

Within the while loop, the program uses a StringTokenizer object to break the line string into pieces separated by white space. These should be integers like "-13" or "25" and are converted to the integer value by using `Integer.parseInt`. Both `readLine` and `Integer.parseInt` can throw exceptions, so we have our second code block inside a try-catch.

We echo the values read from the file to the output area to help illustrate that the program is doing what we expect. Here is the ViewFrame after reading all data from the file IntData.txt:

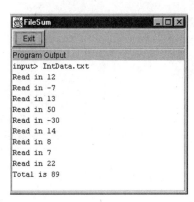

The file IntData.txt would print out as shown below.

```
12   -7  13

50

-30  14
8
                         7
22
```

The continue Statement

Several lines are blank. We handle this in the code with the lines

```
if (st.countTokens() == 0)
    continue;
```

This says that if there are no tokens, then go directly to the while loop's condition and read in another line. The `continue` statement is used in both while and for loops to skip the rest of the body of a loop and start the next iteration. The `break` statement is used to exit a loop immediately. These two statements cause an alteration of the normally expected flow of control of a program, and thus should be used with care. They are appropriate only when code written without their use is significantly more complicated and difficult to understand than code written with them.

We should have closed the file explicitly, but we omitted that step.

File Output

We may wish to write information to a file. The following example, `Coder.java`, illustrates both file output and character-by-character processing. It is a simple example of file encoding. We use the simple Caesar cipher that was illustrated in a prior lab: each alphabetic character is replaced by the next character in the alphabetic sequence, with 'a' replacing 'z'. We convert all upper-case characters to lower case before encoding. For convenience we attach the suffix ".enc" to the file name to indicated the encoded version.

For input we use the `read` method of `BufferedReader`, which returns a character in integer form. Internally characters are stored as unsigned integers, so this isn't a problem. And this allows the method to return `-1` to indicate that it encountered end-of-file and could not read any more characters. For output we use `BufferedWriter` and its method `write`, which takes an integer parameter that is a character.

As usual we must worry about exceptions when opening the files for reading or writing and exceptions thrown by the methods `read` and `write`. The action takes place in the method associated with the `EncodeAction` class.

You can download the two files `Coder.java` and `CoderTest.java` and put them in a project. Compile and run the resulting program. Also download the file `Message.txt` as an example file to encode. We just show Coder.java, as the only thing CoderTest.java does is create an instance of a Coder object.

```java
// Coder.java
// An object that can encode a text file using a simple Caesar cipher. The output
// file's name is the input file's name with the suffix ".enc" appended.

import java.io.*;
import java.awt.event.*;
import java.awt.*;
import javax.swing.*;
import LabPkg.*;

public class Coder
{
    ViewFrame vf;

    public Coder()
    {
        vf = new ViewFrame("Coder");
        vf.setIOEcho(true);
        vf.addActionButton(new EncodeAction("Encode a File"));
        vf.setVisible(true);
    }

    class EncodeAction extends AbstractAction
    {
        public EncodeAction(String s)
        {
            super(s);
        }

        public void actionPerformed(ActionEvent e)
        {
            String fname = vf.readString("Enter the name of the file to encode");
            fname = fname.trim();
            String outFname = fname + ".enc";
            BufferedReader inFile = null;
            BufferedWriter outFile = null;
            int c;
            // try to open the files
            try
            {
                inFile = new BufferedReader(new FileReader(fname));
                outFile = new BufferedWriter(new FileWriter(outFname));
            }
            catch(IOException x)
            {
```

```
                vf.showWarningMsg("Problem opening files: " + x);
                if (inFile != null)
                {
                    try{
                        inFile.close();
                    }catch(Exception z){}
                }
                if (outFile != null)
                {
                  try{
                    outFile.close();
                  }catch(Exception z){}
                }
                System.exit(0);   // could also use return; here
            }
            // files are open so proceed
            try
            {
                while ((c = inFile.read()) != -1)   // -1 signals end-of-file
                {
                    // Typecast the int returned by read to a char
                    char cc = (char)c;
                    if (!Character.isLetter(cc))
                    {
                        outFile.write(c);
                    }
                    else
                    {
                        cc = Character.toLowerCase(cc);
                        if (cc != 'z')
                          cc = (char)(cc + 1);
                        else
                          cc = 'a';
                        outFile.write((int)cc);
                    }
                }
                inFile.close();
                outFile.close();
                vf.println("Encoded file is " + outFname);
            }
            catch(IOException x)
            {
                vf.showWarningMsg("Problem during encoding: " + x);
                vf.println("Kill window after reading message");
            }

        }
    }
}
```

Console I/O

Console was the name given to the keyboard and screen of early computer systems where access was a terminal to a mainframe computer. This was command line input from the keyboard and program output to the screen.

In Java there is a special object that is automatically created and associated with the keyboard input stream: `System.in`. The object `System.out` is automatically associated with the screen.

Output is easy, as `System.out` contains methods `println` and `print` that are like the methods of the same name in ViewFrame. Both methods expect a String parameter and display it on the screen.

To read efficiently from the keyboard, one uses a `BufferedReader` associated with an `InputStreamReader`, which is in turn associated with `System.in`. For example,

```
BufferedReader keybd = new BufferedReader(new InputStreamReader(System.in));
```

The variable `keybd` can be used with methods `readLine` or `read`. The creation doesn't require being in a try-catch clause, as `System.in` automatically exists and so nothing can go wrong. However, `readLine` and `read` can throw exceptions.

The following simple example shows how much work it takes in Java to read in an integer from the keyboard and display whether it is odd or even, without using a graphical user interface.

```java
// ConsoleIODemo.java
// Shows how to read from console keyboard and write to output

import java.io.*;
import java.util.*; // for StringTokenizer

public class ConsoleIODemo
{
    public static void main(String[] args)
    {
        BufferedReader keybd = new BufferedReader(
                            new InputStreamReader(System.in));
        System.out.println("Enter an integer");
        try
        {
            String line = keybd.readLine();
            StringTokenizer st = new StringTokenizer(line);
            if (st.hasMoreTokens())
            {
                int n = Integer.parseInt(st.nextToken());
                if (n % 2 == 0)
                {
                    System.out.println("EVEN");
                }
                else
                {
                    System.out.println("ODD");
                }
            }
            else
            {
                System.out.println("No value was entered");
            }
        }
        catch (IOException e)
        {
            System.out.println("" + e);
            e.printStackTrace();
        }
    }
}
```

You may wish to download the file, compile it, and run it. Your IDE should provide a console window for this kind of output.

The Laboratory

Objectives

- To gain experience reading a file and processing its data.
- To gain experience handling exceptions.

A Guide to the Laboratory

- You will create the file `DoubleSpace.java` in task 1 and modify it in tasks 2 and 3. Turn in copies of all three versions of the file. (Remember to print out a copy at the end of each task!)

■ You are to make a modification to `Coder.java`. You will turn in a printout with your changes.

Task 1: Double Spacing (with a ViewFrame)

Write a program in the file `DoubleSpace.java` that will use a ViewFrame to request the name of a file from the user. Then the program will open the file and send it line by line to the screen with a blank line between every line of the file. You may use the ViewFrame for the output display.

Print out a copy of the file when it is working.

Task 2: Double Spacing (without a ViewFrame)

Write a program in the file `DoubleSpace.java` that will request the name of a file from the user using console input. Then the program will open the file and send it line by line to the screen with a blank line between every line of the file. Use `System.out.println` for output. Do not use a ViewFrame object in the program.

Print out a copy of the file when it is working.

Task 3: Modifying DoubleSpace .java

Further modify the DoubleSpace.java program so that it sends the double-spaced output to a file of the same name as the input file but with the string ".ds" appended. Hence if the input file is named letter.txt, then the output file will be letter.txt.ds.

Print out a copy of the program when it is working.

Task 4: A Fix of Coder.java

The file Coder.java encodes a file using the simple Caesar cipher for letters of the alphabet. Such characters are always converted to lower case. Fix it so the encoding works for upper- or lower-case characters, i.e., maintain the case when you replace the letter by another letter.

Compile and test your results.

Post-Laboratory Exercises

Exercise 1: Decoding

Modify the file `Coder.java` to add a button that *decodes* an encoded file and displays the decoded message in the output area of the ViewFrame object `vf` rather than writing it to a file.

You should be able to test this by first encoding a file and then decoding it.

Exercise 2: Frequency of Letters

Write a program that will request the name of a file, open the file and read its contents, and display in the output area of a ViewFrame object the number of times each letter of the alphabet occurs, ignoring case. *Hint:* Consider an array of 26 cells initialized to 0. The 0-th cell will hold the number of times 'a' or 'A' occurs and the cell at position 25 will hold the number of occurrences of 'z' or 'Z'.

Hint: If c is a character variable holding an upper-case character, then the expression `(int)(c - 'A')` will give the array a position where you can keep the count for the character that c holds.

14

Java GUI Programming

We have been using graphical components in our programming. The package LabPkg has a ViewFrame class that is an extension of JFrame—a class defined in javax.swing. JFrame is an extension of Frame, which was defined in java.awt.

The ViewFrame class allows for the display of a Canvas object and always has a TextArea object for output. It also has a Panel object that contains an Exit button. This has been very useful in elementary programs, but is too restrictive for general use. We need to look at the way Java approaches graphical user interface (GUI) programming. Then we can design a graphical user interface for our application that fits the application and has the correct look and feel.

Java has evolved since its release in early 1994. The first version was available in JDK 1.0 and had a poorly designed GUI system. JDK 1.1 changed how events were handled and made Java more efficient when it came to GUI programming. In 1999 JDK 1.2 extended things to allow more control of the look and feel and more features. For example, in JDK 1.2 a better file-finder dialog was provided in the swing package. This is fundamental in most applications. The swing package used *lightweight components* that enabled a speed up of the repainting process. In the following description of Java GUI programming, we will use only features available in JDK 1.1 and 1.2.

In this laboratory we will start from the basics and create a simple Frame object and add Panels to it. Then we will explore the event handling system and handling mouse events—clicks in a window or mouse movement. The goal is to prepare you for writing event-driven applications like solitaire games.

Pre-Laboratory Reading

What Is the AWT?

The AWT is a set of Java classes that support the graphics of user interfaces. If you want your program to interact with the user via graphical components, you will use classes from the AWT. The AWT is part of the library of classes distributed with the JDK (Java Development Kit).[1] There are other collections of classes that provide similar and sometimes greater functionality, but they may not be installed on every system that has a Java interpreter. An example is the Foundation Classes collection distributed by Netscape. In early 1999 the swing classes from Sun were standardized. These provide somewhat more sophisticated graphical components than are available using the AWT. (See below.)

The AWT, or "Another Window Toolkit," is based on the Component class. The visible graphical classes extend this class. A Component object has information about its size (in pixels),[2] its location on the screen, its foreground and background colors, and so on.

The classes we care about most are the Frame, Panel, Button, Label, Canvas, TextField, and TextArea classes. Both Frame and Panel are *container* classes. That means they can contain other GUI components. A Panel might have several labels and buttons or even other Panel objects. There is a Window class, but Frame is a simple extension of it that contains the usual borders and a title bar. Plus a Frame can have a menu bar attached to it. We normally use Frame rather than Window for our main container.

What Is Swing?

The swing classes were made available in 1999 as part of the package javax.swing. They add new graphical user interface classes and are *lightweight*. By lightweight, we mean that (in a nontechnical sense) they can be visually realized more efficiently. We use swing classes to create the ViewFrame class of the LabPkg package, but an extensive discussion of this package is beyond the scope of this laboratory manual.

What Is Event-Driven Programming?

In graphical user interface programming all program actions are initiated by *events*. An event could be

- a mouse click,
- a mouse pointer entering a component,
- a key press, or
- an action initiated by a program or a hardware component.

The operating system has a special program, the graphics subsystem, that is responsible for displaying graphical information on the screen at the request of user programs. It also informs user programs of events. Once a program starts that has a graphical component, it won't stop until the last component is dis-

---

1. Sun Microsystems refers to this as the SDK for Java 2.
2. A pixel is a "picture element." It refers to a particular dot on the screen. Computer screens are composed of a grid of such dots. A resolution of 1,024 by 760 means that there are 760 rows and 1,024 columns of dots, or 1,024*760 pixels. Each pixel is assigned a color. Changes occur on the screen by repainting selected pixels.

posed of. This means that if a Java program creates a component object such as a Frame, then the program will not terminate, even after all the instructions in the main method are completed, until the Frame is disposed of. Hence, it is important to provide a way to dispose of components. If the Java interpreter is terminated with `System.exit(0)`, then all components are automatically disposed of.

In Java, a Component object must add a special *listener* object that has methods that are called when an event occurs. By "add" we mean that the listener object is associated or registered with the component object and may take action to call methods of the object when an event occurs.

This type of programming, where actions are initiated by external events, is called event-driven programming. It is commonly associated with user interfaces. But a simple room thermostat is an event-driven "program." When the temperature in a room drops below a selected level, the heat turns on. When the temperature rises above a certain level, the heat goes off. The events are changes in temperature.

Threads

A thread, or thread-of-control, is a sequence of computer instructions that execute concurrently with and may share data with other threads. The instructions in the main method of a Java program represent a thread. The graphics support system is a part of the operating system that works with graphics programs. The graphics support system runs as a separate thread from your program; both are executing "simultaneously." When a Component object is created, it activates a thread that checks all events and sends notification to the listeners of the Component object. Your program ends when all the related threads end. If no graphics objects are created, then there is only a single thread—the instructions in the main method of your program.

Sharing a CPU

Your computer typically has a single CPU (central processing unit) that carries out instructions. It is important to understand that threads and whole programs take turns using the CPU. In most computers this is done in a simple round-robin fashion. Since in many cases entire programs can complete in a fraction of a second, if each of 10 threads or programs has the CPU for 1/100th of a second, the user will hardly notice that a thread or program is not running continuously.

Graphics programming is only possible with this combination of threads and sharing of the CPU. Fortunately, most programmers need not know how it works.

Basic GUI Classes

Frame

The Frame class produces a window with a title line and can support a menu bar. It uses the default layout of BorderLayout, which is described in the lab.

HandleWindow Death

A window requires a special listener object that kills the window when you click on the X in the upper-right corner. The HandleWindowDeath class of the LabPkg package will do this. We add the listener object to the Frame object. This is demonstrated in the lab.

Panel	A Panel is a rectangular container that uses FlowLayout. This means that as components are added, they appear from left to right until the width is exhausted and a new row is started. One can specify left or right justification of the components within the panel. The default is to center the components.
Canvas	A Canvas is a simple object for drawing upon or displaying an image upon. It cannot contain other objects. Normally, it is extended and its paint method is overwritten.
Layout	There are three common extensions of the Layout class: BorderLayout, FlowLayout, and GridBagLayout. Layout objects take care of positioning components in a container class like a Panel or a Frame. Each of the three classes that extend Layout uses a different positioning convention.
Button	These are rectangular components that have a label and can react to mouse clicks. The reaction depends on the associated listeners.
AbstractAction	In javax.swing, the AbstractAction class allows one to create an action that also manifests itself as a button object when displayed on a panel. This somewhat simplifies how the AWT handles buttons and their listeners.
Listeners	A *listener* is a special type of object that is registered with the graphics subsystem and associated with a graphics component. When an event occurs to a component, a special method within each of the listener objects registered with the component is called. **By rewriting the special method for the component method, you can control the response to the event.**

Review Questions

1. What is the AWT?
2. What class in the AWT is a visual window with a border and can have a menu bar?
3. What class in the AWT is used to draw on or display images but cannot contain other components?
4. What are examples of events?

The Laboratory

Objectives

- To gain experience using basic components of the AWT.
- To create event-driven applications that respond to mouse events.

A Guide to the Laboratory—A Checklist

This lab requires following a series of steps carefully. The steps are listed below. Use this as a checklist.

- **Step 1:** Download the file HandleWindowDeath.java.
- **Step 2:** Create a project called FirstFrame, and add the file HandleWindowDeath.java to it.

- **Step 3:** Create the new file `SimpleFrame.java` as shown in task 1 and add it to the project. We want to use only basic Java classes that are provided in the awt package, so you will *not* import the LabPkg. Make changes or additions to the file as described in the text following the file listing. When finished, print out a copy of SimpleFrame.java.
- **Step 4:** Close the project above.
- **Step 5:** Create a new project called `MouseDemo` and add the following files to it:
  - HandleWindowDeath.java
  - SimpleFrame.java

  Create the new file `ClickableCanvas.java` described in task 2 and add it to the project. You will add the two lines
  ```
  v.add(p);
  c.repaint();
  ```
  to the `mousePressed` method.
- **Step 6:** In the `paint` method, get an Iterator object and use it to display a text string associated with each point. (See the note in the post-lab section on Vector and Iterator.)
- **Step 7:** Modify `SimpleFrame.java` as indicated at the end of task 2.
- **Step 8:** Rebuild all of the files and run the program. Fix any errors.

Turn in copies of SimpleFrame.java (both versions) and ClickableCanvas.java.

Task 1: Creating a Basic Frame with Border Layout

A Basic Window

We want to define a simple window that will initially have nothing in it.

Create a new Java file called `SimpleFrame.java`. Now in the SimpleFrame.java editing window, enter the code below. The code defines a class that extends the Frame class. **We insert a main method within the class only for initial testing with a single file.** The Constructor actually doesn't do very much and we could leave it off in this example, but since we will be adding to it later we show it.

```java
// SimpleFrame.java
// Programmer(s):     YOUR NAME(s) HERE

import java.awt.*;
import java.awt.event.*;

public class SimpleFrame extends Frame
{
    // Constructor
    //  As an example we simply set the background color
    public SimpleFrame()
    {
        setBackground(Color.yellow);
    }

    // a main to test this class
    public static void main(String[] args)
    {
        // we create an object of type Simple Frame
        SimpleFrame f = new SimpleFrame();
        // we can now set some of its properties using
        // methods of the Frame class
        f.setSize(300,250);
```

```
                                f.setTitle("First SimpleFrame");
                                f.setVisible(true);
                          }
                    }
```

Now save the file and compile it. If there are errors, correct them and compile the file again.

Now run the program. The window should appear on your screen and have a yellow background. Try to terminate the window. It ignores all attempts to kill it. This is because we don't have a listener object to notify the program that we want the window to disappear or destroy itself. Without a listener, the Frame is not getting notification of your requests to kill the window.

How do we get rid of this window?

Your IDE should have an option to terminate the current program. Go ahead and kill the window using this method.

Adding a Listener

The listener class for a window is called `WindowAdapter`. It has methods that are called when a window is iconified, restored, activated, or closed. Closing a window is an event that occurs when the user uses the `Close` option of the menu or clicks on the X in the upper-right corner of a window in the Windows 95/NT/2000 system to kill the window.

We have defined our own class that `extends WindowAdapter` in the package LabPkg. It has our own version of the method called `WindowClosing()`. The name of the class is `HandleWindowDeath` and the file is shown below.

```
//package LabPkg;
// LabPkg is software from "Basic Java Programming - A Laboratory Approach"

// HandleWindowDeath.java
//   a simple class that handles the killing of a window

import java.awt.*;
import java.awt.event.*;

/**
 * a utility class to handle the termination of a window.
 * This class also kills the Java VM.
 * @author J F Kent
 */
public class HandleWindowDeath extends WindowAdapter
{
    public void windowClosing(WindowEvent e)
    {
        // no confirmation, just kill all!
        Window w = e.getWindow();
        w.setVisible(false);
        w.dispose();
        System.exit(0);
    }
}
```

This version is not part of the LabPkg, as we have commented out the package directive on the first line. Add the file to the project and compile it.

Now in the main method for the class `SimpleFrame`, add the line

```
f.addWindowListener(new HandleWindowDeath());
```

after the line where f is created but before its size is set. It actually can be done anywhere after f is created.

Now save and recompile the program. Run it. Kill it with the mouse by selecting `Close` on the pop-up menu that comes up when you click at the upper left of the window border. The program should terminate. If it doesn't, check that you inserted the line `f.addWindowListener(...)`; as indicated above.

Run it again and kill the window by clicking on the X in the upper-right corner of the window. *Remember:* When creating a Frame object or an object of a class that extends Frame, you must add an instance of HandleWindowDeath via the `addWindowListener()` method in order to be able to close (kill) the window.

Adding Components to the Frame

Our window is not very interesting. We usually want to put something in it. The Frame class is a *Container* class. This means that we can add other components to it. How do we indicate where they go within the Frame?

The Layout

All container classes have a LayoutManager that uses a default *layout*. A layout is just a scheme for arranging components within a container. For example, we might want them to appear from left to right in the order in which they were added to the container. If there are too many components added for the width of the container, then a second row is started automatically, then a third, etc. In Java this type of layout is called FlowLayout.

For Frame objects the default layout is `BorderLayout`. A BorderLayout can have components in any of five places designated by "North", "South", "East", "West", and "Center". The diagram below shows the general position of the components of the Frame's layout. Of course, this means that such a layout can

North		
West	Center	East
South		

have at most five components added to it, but each of these could itself be a container so it is not very restrictive. The Center component is usually the significant one. It expands to fill the Frame if the other components are missing.

To show the layout we will add five Panel objects to our SimpleFrame class' layout, each with a different background color. The `add()` method is used to add a component. It takes two parameters—the component and the string that describes where it is to go.

Open the file SimpleFrame.java and comment out the line

```
setBackground(Color.yellow);
```

in the constructor.

Immediately after the line and *inside* the constructor, add the following code, being very careful about the case of the letters.

```
Panel p1 = new Panel();
p1.setBackground(Color.red);
add(p1,"Center");
Panel p2 = new Panel();
p2.setBackground(Color.blue);
```

```
add(p2,"North");
Panel p3 = new Panel();
p3.setBackground(Color.yellow);
add(p3,"South");
Panel p4 = new Panel();
p4.setBackground(Color.green);
add(p4,"East");
Panel p5 = new Panel();
p5.setBackground(Color.cyan);
add(p5,"West");
```

Please note that this code must go *inside* the constructor's braces. We commented out the setting of the background of the Frame, as the five panels will cover it up in any case.

Save the file and compile it and run it. Do you see the layout clearly? Now remove the part of the constructor that refers to p3. Save the file, compile it, and run it. Notice that the center part expands to take the place of the missing "South" component.

The Quit Button

It is often useful to add an explicit Quit button to a window. Such a button causes the program to stop immediately when pressed. We will add such a button to the p2 panel. We will also need to define an `ActionListener` object for the button.

After the creation of p2 (`Panel p2 = new Panel();`) in the constructor, add the following lines:

```
Button quitButton = new Button("Quit Now");
quitButton.addActionListener( new AL() );
quitButton.setBackground(Color.white);
p2.add(quitButton);   // puts the button on the panel p2
```

We also need to define the class AL, which will be a listener for the button. At the end of the file after all the other classes, add the following lines:

```
class AL implements ActionListener
{
    public void actionPerformed(ActionEvent e)
    {
        System.exit(0);
    }
}
```

This *implements* ActionListener, which means that it is a class that contains the method `actionPerformed()`. This method is called when the button is pressed.

Now save and compile the file. Run it. You should see the button in the top or north panel. Clicking on it should terminate the program and the window.

Now print your current version of the `SimpleFrame.java` file and turn it in to show that you've completed this stage of the lab. Be sure your name is on the printout.

Summary

We have seen that to create a graphical object that is a window on your screen you extend the Frame class. You must add a listener to handle the closing of the window.

Arrangement of objects within the window is determined by a layout. BorderLayout is the standard layout for Frame objects, while FlowLayout is the standard layout for Panel objects. For components such as Button objects one must add an actionListener to handle events.

The Swing component JFrame is an extension of Frame. In the package LabPkg we have defined ViewFrame as an extension of it. ViewFrame has a

Panel object in the "North" position and a TextArea object in the "Center" position. If a Canvas object is provided, it is in the "South" position.

Task 2: An Event-Driven Application with a Special Canvas

In this part of the laboratory we want to create a special Canvas extension that displays the position of a mouse click. In fact we will keep track of the previous mouse clicks using a vector and display them all when the window is repainted.

The Canvas will be placed in the Center position of the Frame. We will keep the Panel with the Quit button in the North position.

ClickableCanvas Class

The class will be a Canvas that responds to mouse clicks. To achieve this, we must add a MouseListener to the Canvas. We also will need to get the point where the click occurred and save it in a vector.

Create a project called `MouseDemo` and add the file `SimpleFrame.java` to it. We will modify this file in a few moments. Also add HandleWindowDeath.java to the project. Now open a *new* file and enter the code below.

```
// ClickableCanvas.java
// Your Name(s) here
// Canvas that records mouse-click positions and
// displays the text of the coordinates.

import java.awt.*;
import java.awt.event.*;
import java.util.*;

public class ClickableCanvas extends Canvas
{
    Vector v;

    public ClickableCanvas()
    {
        super();
        v = new Vector();
        addMouseListener(new ML());
    }

    public void paint(Graphics g)
    {
        Dimension d = getSize();
        g.clearRect(0,0,d.width,d.height);
          // more to come
    }
    // inner class
    class ML extends MouseAdapter
    {
        public void mousePressed(MouseEvent e)
        {
            Point p = e.getPoint();
            // more to come
        }
    }
}
```

MouseListener is the class `ML`, which extends `MouseAdaptor`. We only revise the `MousePressed` method that is called when a mouse click occurs in the canvas. The `Point` object p has two public data members, `p.x` and `p.y`, which are the coordinates of the point on the canvas where the click occurred. We want to save this point by adding it to the vector v and then repaint the canvas. This is done by inserting the following two lines in the `MousePressed` method:

```
v.add(p);
repaint();
```

Now in the paint method we want to display each point in text form on the canvas. This means we get an Iterator of the vector v. Each element returned by the iterator's `next` method is cast to a Point object. We could draw the String "(45,128)" if the Point had data members 45 and 128.

Complete the `paint` method. You will need to get an Iterator object to access the points in the Vector v. **Refer to the post-laboratory reading for how to do this.** Save the file and compile it to check for simple errors.

Now open `SimpleFrame.java` and revise it as shown below. We want only one Panel. It will have a Quit button and be in the "North" position. We want a ClickableCanvas object in the "Center" position. Eliminate the other code about Panels.

```java
// SimpleFrame.java
// YOUR NAME(S) HERE
// We create a simple extension of Frame with
// a Quit button and a Clickable Canvas.

import java.awt.*;
import java.awt.event.*;
import LabPkg.*;          // to get HandleWindowDeath class

public class SimpleFrame extends Frame
{
    ClickableCanvas c;
    // Constructor
    public SimpleFrame()
    {
        addWindowListener(new HandleWindowDeath()); // here rather
                                                    // than in main

        Panel p = new Panel();
        p.setBackground(Color.gray);
        Button quitButton = new Button("Quit Now");
        quitButton.addActionListener(new AL());
        quitButton.setBackground(Color.white);
        p.add(quitButton);  // puts the button on the panel p
        add(p,"North");
        c = new ClickableCanvas();
        c.setBackground(Color.yellow);
        add(c, "Center");
    }


    // inner class
    class AL implements ActionListener
    {
        public void actionPerformed(ActionEvent e)
        {
            System.exit(0);
        }
    }

    // a main method to create an instance of a Simple Frame
    public static void main(String[] args)
    {
        Frame f = new SimpleFrame();
        f.setSize(300,250);
        f.setTitle("SimpleFrame with ClickableCanvas");
        f.setVisible(true);
    }

}
```

Save the file. Compile it. Run it. When you have finished, print out a copy of `ClickableCanvas.java` to turn in.

Post-Laboratory Exercises and Reading

Exercise

Modify the `ClickableCanvas` class so that the `paint` method draws a line from each mouse-click point to the one that follows it in the vector, with the newest point at the end of the last line segment. Add a "Clear" button to the panel next to the "Quit" button that resets the vector of points to empty by calling a method of ClickableCanvas. Call the method `clearHistory()`. Check the Vector class documentation to find a method in the Vector class that empties the vector.

Vector and Iterator Notes

You may wish to look back at the laboratory "Collections" for its material on Vectors and the laboratory "Drawing with Java" for its material on Iterators.

Given a Vector v, the action

```
Iterator i = v.iterator();
```

provides an Iterator object. Actually, Iterator is an interface containing the methods

```
hasNext()
next()
```

The former returns a boolean value while the latter gives an object from the vector. A typical use might look like

```
while (i.hasNext())
{
    Point p = (Point)i.next(); // note the explicit type cast
    // do something with the p object

}
```

where we assume that the Vector contained Point objects.

In the ClickableCanvas class' `paint` method you will want to use the Graphics method `drawString()`. A typical use might look like

```
g.drawString("Message", 75, 125);
```

which would display the given string at the point (75,125) using the font and color of the Graphics object g.

You will want to print out "(25,35)" at the Point p representing (25,35). Recall that p.x and p.y will give the values of the coordinates of p. Then the string would be

```
"(" + p.x + "," + p.y + ")"
```

LABORATORY **15**

Solitaire Games

In event-driven programming, the "action" of a program occurs in the methods called when events occur. A perfect example of this is a computer game like solitaire where the user has the mouse move cards from pile to pile. The events are the mouse clicks. The responses are card movements and repainting of parts of the visible game board.

We have sufficient knowledge after completing the previous laboratories to write our own version of the game FreeCell. It will not be as polished as the game that is available on many computers because we don't know how to use double-buffering to avoid some flickering when repainting and because we won't use real card images—our cards will indicate suit and rank but will not be the traditional images of real playing cards.

The key to success in writing the fairly large program ahead of us is careful design and planning. We must determine what classes will be needed, what methods each class will support, and the extent to which we will use inheritance or interfaces when we relate classes with common features. We must be able to test the classes as we develop them. We also must understand the rules of the game that we will program.

The pre-laboratory reading explores the design and organizational issues ahead. The laboratory examines the classes and the program files and does simple testing along the way. Our goal is to show that although the task is large in comparison to previous efforts, it is manageable.

The laboratory is divided into two sessions. The first session explores and tests code for the Card class and the classes that extend CardPile. It develops a new class that extends CardPile and tests it. The second session looks at the complete FreeCell game and adds a feature.

It is critically important that the code for the classes be read carefully.

Special Task

Before reading further, you will want to download, or copy, the files used in this laboratory from the diskette provided. There are quite a few of them. They should be placed in a special subfolder called `FreeCellFiles` that is in your folder `Z:\lab_files`. Be sure to create this subfolder before you start the download. This will avoid confusion with earlier versions of the files that might not be complete or could have errors.

Pre-Laboratory Reading

The FreeCell Game

Solitaire has hundreds of variations. A traditional version is called *Klondike*. In that version seven rows of cards are dealt out. In each row all the cards except the top one are face down. The first row has one card, the next row has two cards, the next has three cards, and so on. After the rows are dealt out, cards are examined from the remaining cards in the deck, usually one at a time. The goal is to get all of the cards into four piles—one pile per suit, in ascending order starting with the ace.

The picture below shows a Klondike computer game. The first card in the

deck, a 6 of hearts, has been turned over. Several moves are possible. For example, the 6H could be moved to the 7C (7 of clubs). Also, the 3S could be moved to the 4D. If the 3S was moved, its row would be empty. In such a case, any top card that was a king could be moved to the empty spot. So we could move the KD (king of diamonds) to that spot. When a row has no face up cards, its top card may be turned over.

The general rule in Klondike is that in the vertical rows (called tableau piles), a new card can be placed on top of the pile if it is the opposite color and is the next face value or rank in descending order. If an ace is available as a top face up card, it could be immediately moved to one of the four empty piles at the upper-right to start a suit pile. By a suit pile, we mean a card pile that is all the same suit and in ascending order: ace, 2, 3, 4,..., queen, king.

Microsoft's FreeCell   *FreeCell* is the solitaire game we want to program. A picture of an electronic version[1] is shown below. The upper left has four empty piles that are allowed

to have at most one card placed on them. These are the "free cells" used in the game. Notice that the deck is completely distributed into eight rows, or tableau piles, with all cards facing up. The rules are the same as for Klondike except there is no deck to work with. Several moves are immediately available and are listed in order below. They are not necessarily the best moves, just examples:

- 7S to 8H
- 6H to 7S
- 5S to 6H
- JS to a free cell
- Ace of spades or clubs (we can't see which until the cards are physically moved) to a suit pile

We will create our own version of this computer game using the same rules but our own graphics. Our focus will be on a design that makes use of object-oriented programming and supports the reuse of classes in other computer card games.

The Design of Our FreeCell Program

Looking at the game board shows what we need to have in any solitaire game design:

- a class for a Card object that can be drawn/displayed either face up or face down
- a class for a collection or pile of cards that maintains the cards in an appropriate order
- a class for the game board on which the card piles and their cards will be displayed
- a window to contain the game board and perhaps have button or menu options for quitting or starting a new game
- a class that encapsulates the "game"

---

1. The electronic version shown below is copyrighted by Microsoft 1981–1996 and is written by Jim Horne.

- a mechanism that allows us to move cards from pile to pile according to the rules of the game

The last component is where event-driven programming enters the picture. **The mechanism will be the methods that respond to mouse events.**

A simple design combines the "game" class and the "window" class. Essentially a FreeCell object will be a specialized Frame object that will create (in its constructor) a "game board" and add it in the center of the window.

The game board will be a specialized Canvas where we can draw Card and CardPile objects. In its constructor, the board will be laid out. It will have listeners for mouse clicks. The response to mouse clicks will be the mechanism that can make legal moves of cards from pile to pile.

Let's consider the classes in turn and discuss each of their characteristics. Remember that we want to be able to write code for each class.

The Card Class

The Card class is fundamental to all computer card games. To develop a Card class we have to think of

- What data is needed to maintain the state of a particular card?
- What methods are required to access and modify the data and display the card on the computer screen?

Data Fields

There are two obvious characteristics of a playing card:

- suit (diamond, heart, spade, or club)
- rank (ace, 2, 3, ..., 10, jack, queen, or king)

For use in a computer game we also need to know if a card is face up or face down and its position on the board.

The background color of the card is also useful. Its foreground color is determined by its suit (red or black). The physical size of the card is needed to determine how much of the screen it covers, and it allows one to check if a particular location is inside the card's space. The latter is important when asking if a particular mouse click occurred on the card.

Hence, it makes sense to declare the following components:

```
protected boolean faceup;
protected int r;  // rank
protected int s;  // suit
protected int x = 0;  // location of card image rectangle
protected int y = 0;
protected Color bg = Color.white;
protected int width = Card.WIDTH;
protected int height = Card.HEIGHT;
```

It is useful to have some number codes for the suits and ranks. These are much easier to work with than strings. The following definitions are *constants,* as they are declared *final.*

```
// public constants for default width and height of a card
final public static int WIDTH = 60;
final public static int HEIGHT = 90;
// codes for the suits
final public static int HEART = 1;
final public static int SPADE = 2;
final public static int DIAMOND = 3;
final public static int CLUB = 4;
// Codes for the ranks. Non-face cards and non-aces have
// their normal rank value, i.e., a 5 of hearts has rank 5.
final public static int ACE = 1;
final public static int KING = 13;
```

```
final public static int QUEEN = 12;
final public static int JACK = 11;
```

The fact that they are static means they can be used in situations like

```
int r = c.getRank(); // c is a Card object
int s = c.getSuit();
if (r == Card.ACE && s == Card.SPADE) // c is ace of spades
{
    ....
}
```

Methods

Of course we will need constructors for creating Card objects. At a minimum these will provide the rank and suit desired and the location. The dimensions can be omitted, and the values Card.WIDTH and Card.HEIGHT used.

We will want access methods like

- `getSuit`
- `getRank`
- `getLocation`
- `setLocation`

After a card is created it won't change its suit or rank but it could change its position on the board. So we will provide a setLocation method, but no setRank or setSuit methods.

The user will also want to check whether the card is face up or face down. A method `isFaceUp` will return true if the card is face up and false if it is face down. A method `flip` will turn the card over. As mentioned above, it will be useful to know if a particular point (x,y) is in the area of the card. A boolean method `includesPoint` will take care of this. **The most important method is one that will cause the card to display itself on the screen.** This is the `draw` method. It will have a Graphics object as its parameter.

How should the `draw` method work?

It should check whether the card is face up or face down. If it is face down it should draw the image of the back of a card at the card's location. If it is face up it should draw an image of the card showing its rank and suit information. (If we used a card image, we would use the Graphics method `drawImage()`.)

Java provides support for displaying images, such as pictures of real cards, but displaying such images efficiently to avoid flickering and delays in display requires familiarity with concepts such as double buffering and clipping. These are beyond the necessary scope of this lab and can be avoided by using basic drawing techniques developed in earlier labs. (We will still have some flickering, but it will be minimal.)

We will make use of the picture component classes we developed in the laboratory "Drawing with Java." Recall that the classes Diamond, Spade, Heart, and Club were developed in the post-lab exercises. If you didn't development them, don't worry, they will be provided.

We will represent a face-up card by a rectangle with its rank written in the upper-left corner and a suit symbol in the middle of the card. We will create and use a special class, CardBack, that represents the back of a card. This will require two data declarations:

```
// We will need to draw the front and back of the card so
// we use the classes that implement PictureComponent.
protected PictureComponent suitPicture;
protected PictureComponent backPicture;
```

Recall that `PictureComponent` is an interface that includes the methods `draw` and `drawFilled`. Each of the classes Diamond, Heart, Spade, Club, and CardBack will implement this interface and can be "drawn." **The PictureComponent objects have positions and dimensions, so they must be changed whenever a card's position is changed.** Hence, we actually create and assign them in the `setLocation` method.

If you have not done so, you should download the files
- Card.java
- CardBack.java

to a special folder FreeCellFiles inside the current working folder. Open them in the IDE and print and read them.

The Web page for downloading the files for the lab has a link to the documentation for all of the classes used in this lab. Read the documentation for the Card class before reading the file Card.java.

We could have you write the Card class, but it is relatively simple—just long and tedious. There are other, more interesting, challenges in the game. Be sure you understand all the methods, including the constructors. We will test our Card class during the laboratory session.

Window = FreeCell Class

The class `FreeCell` will *extend Frame*. Thus, when you create a FreeCell object, you automatically create a window for the game to be played in.

What should the window contain? The central component will be a `FreeCellBoard`, which is discussed in the next section. It is an extension of Canvas, upon which the game is drawn. By "central" we mean that it will be added to the normal layout at the "Center" position.

If we want buttons for quitting or for restarting the game, we can put them on a Panel object in the "North" position. Of course, we will have to be sure that we have a `HandleWindowDeath` object to listen for the killing of the window. Plus we will need listeners for each button. The FreeCellBoard will have its own mouse listeners.

The Game Board

We will call this `FreeCellBoard`. It will extend the Canvas class. Basically, it will operate as follows:
- Its constructor will create the various card piles and position them. **These piles are data components of the class.**
- Its `paint` method will call the `draw` methods for each pile.
- It will have a listener for mouse clicks. The response to each click will be to determine if the click occurred on a card pile and if so, on which pile. We will not support the dragging of a card from one pile to another. To move a card one will click on it, then click again on the destination pile. If the card is a top card, then it may be moved. If the destination pile can accept it, the card will be moved, otherwise the move will be aborted. After any move the `repaint` method will be called to show the new positions.

The CardPile Class

We want to think of piles or stacks of cards as objects. As objects they can have positions on the game board and can accept new cards and have cards removed using methods. However, there are a number of different types of card piles that occur:

- a deck with all cards face down, with the only possible move being the removal of cards
- a tableau pile with some cards face up and special rules for adding and removing cards
- a suit pile where all cards must be a common suit and the ranks must be in ascending order starting with the ace
- singleton piles that can hold at most one card, as in the FreeCell piles

All the piles could be implemented in a common way but impose their restrictions in their methods. This is the essence of inheritance.

The methods of card piles will include methods to

- draw the pile,
- add a card,
- remove a top card,
- indicate if a particular card can be added, and
- indicate if a particular card is the top card.

Furthermore, most piles should be able to indicate if a point occurs in the pile, given the point, and be able to return the top-most card containing the point.

These methods will be discussed as we look at the subclasses of CardPile.

The Class Relationships

The diagrams below show the information in and relationship among the classes in the program.

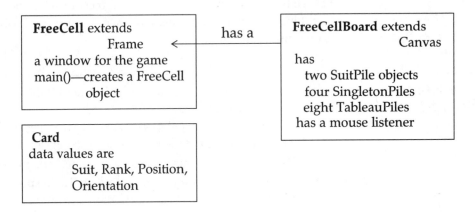

FreeCell extends
        Frame
a window for the game
main()—creates a FreeCell
        object

has a ⟵

FreeCellBoard extends
        Canvas
has
    two SuitPile objects
    four SingletonPiles
    eight TableauPiles
has a mouse listener

Card
data values are
        Suit, Rank, Position,
        Orientation

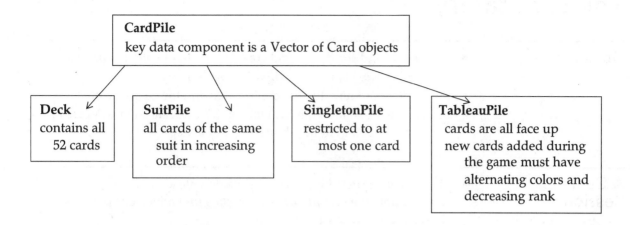

Review Questions

Before proceeding, try to answer the following questions. You may want to reread the pre-lab material and some of the code. The material in the lab on "Java GUI Programming" may also be helpful.

1. Explain the meaning of an "is a" relationship in object-oriented programming.

2. If c is a Card object, what method will fix the position of the card?

3. If c is a Card object, what are the key data components?

4. In CardPile the key data component is a Stack, which is a class that extends _____?

5. Where does the initial layout of the game occur?

6. What does it mean to say a data component is "final"?

7. What is the distinction among the adjectives public, protected, and private?

8. What does "event-driven" programming mean?

9. A Frame object needs to have what type of listener associated with it?

10. A Button object needs to have what type of listener associated with it?

11. From a Vector object, one can create an Enumeration object. What does an Enumeration object do for us? What are its two key methods?

12. CardPile is an abstract class. What makes it so? Why would we want it to be abstract?

13. What is the orientation of all cards in a Deck object? (Read the code for Card.java and Deck.java.)

14. What are the default dimensions of all Card objects?

15. A Card object that is a spade must contain a Spade object that can be drawn. In what method is this object created? Why?

16. What are the restrictions on a SingletonPile object?

17. What are the restrictions on a TableauPile object?

18. What are the restrictions on a SuitPile object?

19. When is a FreeCell game over?

The Laboratory

Objectives	■ To understand the design and creation of a large software project.
	■ To better understand event-driven programming.
	■ To create something that is sophisticated and fun to play with.
	■ To lay the foundation for introducing more advanced ideas in GUI programming, such as double-buffering and images.

A Guide to Session 1	■ Task 1 will create a project containing downloaded files and use it to demonstrate the display of the Card class for various Card objects. There is nothing to turn in.
	■ Task 2 will create a project containing downloaded files and use it to examine the display of card piles and various problems that can occur.
	■ Task 3 will ask you to create a new class called DiscardPile and test it. You will need to turn in a printout of the file DiscardPile.java.

Task 1: Testing the Card Class

Although the entire program for the game is provided, we will want to follow the development steps of the program.

The first class that was developed was the Card class. The goal was the creation of a class that could be used in any computer card game, yet did not rely on images. We used a simple system to display a card's rank and suit. A simple test is to create several cards and display them on a Canvas object that is part of a ViewFrame. This does not test all the methods but does test the drawing of the cards and the changing of their orientation.

Create a project called `CardDisplaying`. It requires that you add the following files to it:

- Card.java
- CardBack.java
- CardTest.java
- Circle.java
- Club.java
- Diamond.java
- Heart.java
- Spade.java
- Triangle.java
- PictureComponent.java

The key test file is `CardTest.java`. Open it and look at `main()`. The file creates four Card objects at various positions. It then draws them on a Canvas object. After a pause it changes their orientation (flips them over) and redraws them.

What are the four positions of the Card objects?

Answer: _____

Compile all of the files and then run the program. Modify the test file to create two other cards

- a 5 of spades

- a 10 of diamonds

and locate them to the right of the current four cards in a new column that is 30 pixels to the right of the current right-most cards. Unlike the other cards, initially draw them face up, then flip them over.

Compile and test the code. You may wish to uncomment the last two parameters of the first four cards. These give different dimensions to the cards. This is not critical, but recompile and examine the results. (Beware—the larger cards may cover part of the two cards you added unless you reposition them.)

Print out a copy of CardTest.java to turn in. Put your name on it.

Task 2: Testing the CardPile Class

Close the current CardDisplaying project. Create a new project called `CardPileDisplaying`. It will allow us to test the classes that are subclasses of CardPile.

Add the following files to the project:
- Card.java
- CardBack.java
- CardPile.java
- CardPileTest.java
- Deck.java
- SuitPile.java
- TableauPile.java
- SingletonPile.java
- PictureComponent.java
- Circle.java
- Triangle.java
- Heart.java
- Spade.java.
- Club.java
- Diamond.java

The `CardPile` class is provided as the parent class for any card pile used in a solitaire-like game. It is "abstract" because its constructor is not public. Thus only its subclasses can call its constructor via the `super` method.

CardPile has two primary data components:
- the position where it will be drawn
- a `Stack` object, which contains its cards

Java provides Stack as an extension of Vector. Hence, it is really a Vector with some additional methods provided. It behaves like a stack of cafeteria trays. You remove the top card when a card is removed, and you put any additions on the top. **It truly behaves like a pile where the only access is via the top.** Such an organization is sometimes called LIFO for last-in, first-out. In the data structures class we examine the possible implementations of classes that exhibit this behavior.

We are primarily interested in the subclasses that extend CardPile. They are
- Deck
- SingletonPile
- SuitPile
- TableauPile

The last is the only one that is complicated and that is only because the cards are in a staggered positioned in the display. Hence, the setting of a card's location and the determination of a pile's visible region require some arithmetic.

The Deck class represents a standard deck of 52 cards. Its constructor creates the cards using a loop within a loop—one giving suit and the other giving rank. It has one new method—shuffle—which randomizes the cards within the Stack. There is another method for debugging that will display all the cards in the deck on "standard output," i.e., using `System.out.println()`.

Take a few minutes to examine the following files in turn and note their methods. Note what restrictions they impose. They make use of methods from `Card.java` in many cases.

- Deck.java
- SingletonPile.java
- SuitPile.java
- TableauPile.java

Now open the file `CardPileTest.java` and read `main()`. You will notice that some parts are commented out. However, the code shows that we will display a string on our ViewFrame's canvas plus 13 card piles. We will create three arrays: one of SingletonPile objects, one of SuitPile objects, and one of TableauPile objects.

Take a minute and consider the rectangle as representing the canvas. In that rectangle indicate the positions of each of the 13 piles. Give the (x,y) values.

After all the piles are created, they are initially empty. A Deck object d is created and shuffled, and then all its cards are removed and distributed to the other piles. The singleton piles are not given any cards, and the suit piles are given a card only if they can accept it. Of course a suit pile cannot accept any cards initially except an ace. If the aces are near the bottom of the deck, it may be the case that no additional cards will be added. At this point, compile the entire project. Then run it.

There is a message at the lower-left corner of the canvas. Notice that after four seconds the message at the lower left changes.

Because redrawing a string doesn't automatically "erase" the previously drawn string, we must clear away the old string by computing a rectangle that contains it and calling the clearRect method of a Graphics object. The only tricky part is that letters like 'g' and 'p' and 'y' drop below the baseline. The distance below the baseline is called the *descent* of the font. The height above the baseline of a letter like 'T' is called the *ascent* of the font. The code below "erases" a string drawn at the point (10, dim.height - 10). This is 10 pixels from the left and 10 pixels from the bottom of the canvas. It is the left-most end of the baseline for the string.

```
FontMetrics fm = g.getFontMetrics();
int w = fm.stringWidth(s);
int ascent = fm.getAscent();
int descent = fm.getDescent();
g.clearRect(10, dim.height - 10 - ascent, w, ascent + descent);
```

The FontMetrics class contains all the key information about the current font. Its methods can tell us how many pixels wide is a given string and what are the values of the ascent and descent for the font. Recall that the rectangle's position is determined by its *upper-left corner*. Try to draw a picture to help you understand the arithmetic.

Uncomment the rest of main that is between /* and */. Then uncomment the line

```
vf.repaint();
```

and recompile the file. Run it.

It moves four cards to the singleton piles but (unfortunately) leaves their images at their old positions. This problem can be solved by commenting out vf.repaint(); and using c.repaint(); instead. The repaint of the canvas clears it completely. However, it turns out that the code to redraw the piles executes before the repainting is fully finished and we lose part of the image. Recompile and run this. See the problem!

This can be fixed with a pause before the redrawing occurs. So uncomment the line

```
Useful.pause(20);
```

along with c.repaint(); and recompile and run the program.

Moral

This is crude because we didn't create a custom Canvas class where the drawing occurs in the paint() method. We will see in our game that the various card piles will be created in the Canvas subclass called FreeCellBoard and drawn there. This solves timing problems.

Task 3: The DiscardPile Class

You are to write and test a class called DiscardPile that will extend CardPile. It has the following rules:

- all cards must be face up

- the cards are stacked vertically and are not staggered
- any card may be added, but only to the top
- only a top card can be removed

Insert the proper JavaDoc-style comments.

You may reuse the `CardPileDisplaying` project, but remove `CardPileTest.java` and replace it with `DiscardPileTest.java`. For `DiscardPileTest.java`, use the `XXXXXXXX.java` template file (available from previous labs) and replace all occurrences of XXXXXXXX (eight upper-case X characters) with `DiscardPileTest`. Then do a "Save As" using the name `DiscardPileTest.java`. Have the Button label changed to "Discard a Card."

The constructor should create a simple Canvas object and modify the ViewFrame creation so its constructor is passed the Canvas object. Be sure to set the size of the Canvas object initially to ViewFrame.WIDTH, ViewFrame.HEIGHT * 2 / 3. It should also create a DiscardPile and a Deck and locate the Deck object at (10,10) and the DiscardPile object at (100,10). When the button is clicked remove a card from the top of the deck and add it to the discard pile and then draw each pile.

Once this is working, print out a copy to turn in. Be sure your name is on it. At this point you should close the project. This ends Session 1 of the laboratory.

A Guide to Session 2

You will compile and run the complete program that provides a version of the FreeCell game. This is basically to illustrate that our design works properly.

Your task will be to make a modification to the code that allows the movement of a block of cards from one tableau pile to another.

The Game at Last!

Create a project called `FreeCellTest` and add the following files to it:

- Card.java
- CardBack.java
- CardPile.java
- Circle.java
- Club.java
- Deck.java
- Diamond.java
- FreeCell.java
- FreeCellBoard.java
- HandleWindowDeath.java
- Heart.java
- PictureComponent.java
- SingletonPile.java
- SuitPile.java
- TableauPile.java
- Triangle.java

The two key files are
- `FreeCellBoard.java`—the canvas on which we will display the game
- `FreeCell.java`—the window that will contain the game canvas and some buttons

We will examine the two files to understand their parts. (Print copies to take notes on if you like.)

FreeCellBoard

This is an extension of Canvas. It has a mouse listener similar to the one used in ClickableCanvas. **This listener is where all the action is.**

Fundamentally the class has two key parts:
- its layout
- its response to mouse events

Components and Layout Issues

Read the comments at the beginning of the file. Look at the layout diagram. Do your own arithmetic and see if the positioning seems correct. (This will take a little time and study. Ask questions if you are confused.)

Notice that, just as in the test code for CardPile, we have arrays of several types of card piles. (You may wish to re-read CardPileTest.java.) The constructor is long and somewhat dull but you should understand what is going on. The purpose of the `allPiles` array is really for simplicity in checking for mouse clicks in a pile without having three separate loops—one for each pile type.

Mouse Listener

Our mouse listener is quite complicated. **This is where the game is played.** It makes use of the key boolean data component `moveInProgress` because a move of a card is a two-step process.
- Step 1: Click on the card you wish to move.
- Step 2: Click on the top card of the destination pile.

Several things can abort a move:
- clicking outside of any pile
- trying an illegal move
- making an initial click on an empty pile
- clicking on any card other than the top card in a pile

The `mousePressed` method gets the position of the click and tries to determine what was intended.

Read this carefully to see if you understand all the cases.
- Outline the cases considered.
- Write out your questions!

The FreeCell Class

Open the file `FreeCell.java`.

This is really quite simple. It extends Frame so it is a stand-alone window. We simply put the `main` method in it because `main` has to go somewhere. All `main` does is create an instance of this class and make it visible. The frame has a Panel with two buttons and a FreeCellBoard canvas object. The usual window listener is added. A single ActionListener serves both buttons, as it is possible to tell which button was pressed.

Don't worry about the technical code for setting a special font or for replacing the canvas when a new game is desired. We could have omitted this, but it makes the game nicer.

Testing the Initial Version of the Game

At this point rebuild all the files and run the program. Play the game. Try some illegal moves.

At this point the program is complete. You may wish to get rid of calls to `displayMessage()` inside `FreeCellBoard.java`, as they are primarily for debugging.

Your Task— Adding a Move

In most solitaire games you are allowed to move part of one tableau pile to another tableau pile, provided the following hold:
- the tableau pile from the card clicked on upwards is in alternating color and decreasing rank order
- the bottom card of the part of the tableau pile that is to be moved is acceptable as the new top card of the destination tableau pile

A degenerate case is the movement of a single card from one tableau pile to another.

You are to modify the file FreeCellBoard.java to allow this move. *Hint:* In order to move a "stack" of cards, you may wish to create a temporary `Stack` object to hold the cards being moved. The idea is simple.
- create a Stack object tempStack
- until the bottom card of the stack that is being moved has been processed
  - take a card from the source pile
  - push the card on (add it to) tempStack
- until tempStack is empty
  - take a card from tempStack
  - add it to the destination pile

You may wish to use a Vector or an array instead of a Stack. Just make sure things end up in the correct order.

Test your code. This may take many plays of the game to cover most cases. Turn in a printout of the modified file `FreeCellBoard.java` with key changes marked in the margins.

Post-Laboratory Exercises

Designing a Blackjack Game

Blackjack is a common computer game. The computer will be the dealer and will play according to a fixed set of rules that are known to the human player.

Read up on Blackjack and design the classes for a computer version.

LABORATORY 16

Klondike

This laboratory assumes that you have completed the laboratory "Solitaire Games." That laboratory focuses on the design of a version of solitaire called FreeCell. If well-designed using object-oriented principles, the classes should be reusable in other card games. We will illustrate this by asking you to write the solitaire game commonly called Klondike.

The Laboratory

Objectives	▪ To illustrate the reuse of classes.
	▪ To gain experience in modifying large programs.

A Guide to the Laboratory

You will want to work within the folder FreeCellFiles that you used in the "Solitaire Games" laboratory.

You will create two key files: `Klondike.java` and `KlondikeBoard.java`. These are the two files that must be turned in when the lab is completed.

Recalling the Game of Klondike

Unlike FreeCell, Klondike has tableau piles with most cards face down and has no free cells or SingletonPiles. It does use that part of a deck that was not distributed to the tableau piles. It has a DiscardPile that holds cards turned over from the deck.

The picture below shows a Klondike computer game. The first card in the

deck, a 6 of hearts, has been turned over. Several moves are possible. For example, the 6H could be moved to the 7C (7 of clubs). Also, the 3S could be moved to the 4D. If the 3S was moved, its row would be empty. In such a case any top card that was a king could be moved to the empty spot. So we could move the KD (king of diamonds) to that spot. When a row has no face up cards, its top card may be turned over.

The SuitPiles work exactly the same as in FreeCell and are in the upper right. As usual the game is over when all of the cards are in the four SuitPiles or the player resigns.

There are some changes from the FreeCell game:

▪ The initial layout has a deck (with some cards removed), an empty discard pile, four empty suit piles across the top row, and seven TableauPiles in a second row. The tableau piles have only the top card facing up. The left-most tableau pile has a single card, the next one has two cards, the next has three cards, and so on. When the game is set up, a Deck object is created and shuffled and then its cards are placed in the tableau piles.

- A click on the deck causes its top card to be turned over and put on top of the discard pile. (This is a complete "move.")
- When the deck is empty and the discard pile is not empty, a click on the discard pile will cause all of its cards to be placed back on the deck.
- A click on any top card in a tableau pile that is face down causes it to be flipped over. (This is a complete "move.")
- Cards cannot be moved from a tableau or suit pile to the discard pile.
- Cards cannot be added to the deck as part of a move.
- The usual rules apply to adding a card to a suit pile and a tableau pile. (We do allow the "block" move from one tableau pile to another that was your task to write in the "Solitaire Games" laboratory.)

Getting Started

On the Web page for downloading files for this laboratory is an applet version of Klondike. You can run it to get a feel for the way the game works. (This version doesn't support block moves among tableau piles.)

Create a project called KlondikeTest and add the following files to it:

- Card.java
- CardBack.java
- CardPile.java
- Circle.java
- Club.java
- Deck.java
- Diamond.java
- DiscardPile.java
- HandleWindowDeath.java
- Heart.java
- PictureComponent.java
- Spade.java
- SuitPile.java
- TableauPile.java
- Triangle.java

We will add two more files—KlondikeBoard.java and Klondike.java—that are based on FreeCell.java and FreeCellBoard.java.

Now use the editor to open `FreeCell.java` and make the necessary modifications to convert it to `Klondike.java`; i.e., edit it and then save it as `Klondike.java`. Of course, the extension of Canvas that you will use will be called `KlondikeBoard`. Add this new file to the project.

Now open `FreeCellBoard.java` and use the editor to replace all occurrences of "FreeCellBoard" with "KlondikeBoard" and then do a "Save As" using the name `KlondikeBoard.java`.

At this point you could try and compile the project and it would work except for not knowing about SingletonPile (notice that it is not part of the project). It would still really be FreeCell because we haven't changed

- the layout
- the responses to mouse clicks that are specific to the new game

Now you must carefully make changes, starting with the layout of the cards and then the distribution of cards from the Deck object to the tableau piles. After the layout and card distribution parts are working, try to make the moves work. Take your time and TEST, TEST, TEST as you go.

When finished, provide your instructor with copies of Klondike.java and KlondikeBoard.java.

Post-Laboratory Reading and Exercises

Applets

Applets are application windows that reside on a Web page. Any application that has its action occur in a Frame or in an extension of a Frame can be converted to an applet in about four minutes. Print out a copy of `FreeCellApplet.java` and compare it with `FreeCell.java`. Key changes are

- `main` is removed (it is handled by the browser code)
- `import java.awt.applet.*;` is added
- the constructor code is replaced by code in an method called `init()` (any constructor parameters are passed in the applet HTML tag)
- window listeners are not needed, nor are titles (the Quit button also will not function, but we forgot to remove it)
- on a Web page in the same directory as the class files, is put the HTML code

```
<applet archive = "solitaire.jar"
    code = "FreeCellApplet.class"
    width = 680
    height = 600>
Problem here! You should not see this if the program runs!
</applet>
```

The phrase `archive = "solitaire.jar"` is not necessary, but causes the program to load faster. You can use your IDE to create this "jar" archive, which contains all the `.class` files of the project. If it is not used then each of the 15 or so `.class` files is loaded across the network separately, slowing down the start-up. Note that the Java source code files are not used—just the compiled (`.class`) files.

If you don't know HTML, most IDEs will create a default page for an applet when you try to run the project. You can then edit that to add other information.

Exercise

Convert your Klondike program to an applet. Don't bother to create Klondike.jar.

APPENDIX A

The LabPkg Package

Overview

A package is a collection of classes usually maintained in a folder with the package name or in an archive file. For user-provided packages, Java expects that the ClassPath environmental variable indicates where to find the files.

This package uses features from Java's `javax.swing` package, so it must be used with Java version 1.2 or later.

Documentation

This package, LabPkg, has its documentation online. The initial page is shown below.

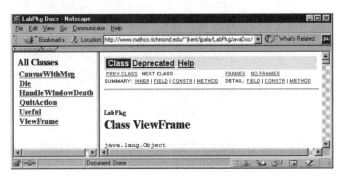

The documentation is accessible via the HTML file

`A:\docs\index.html`

when the diskette provided with the text is inserted into the floppy drive. The URL

`file:///A:/docs/index.html`

will open the file in a browser.

The Classes

There are six classes. Here they are in order of importance:

- `ViewFrame`: A window that supports input and output via simple methods and can display an optional Canvas object. This extends JFrame, which is provided in Java 1.2 as part of the javax.swing package.

- `Die`: A simple class that provides random integers in the range from 1 to N where N is a designated positive integer.
- `Useful`: A class of static methods, the main one being `pause()`.
- `CanvasWithMsg`: An extension of Canvas that displays a simple string centered on the canvas.
- `HandleWindowDeath`: A listener class used by ViewFrame to enable a window to be destroyed when it is closed.
- `QuitAction`: Another listener class used to destroy a ViewFrame window when its Exit button is clicked.

The first three classes are the only ones we will discuss in this appendix.

ViewFrame

Java requires exception handling for input operations. The discussion of exceptions is an advanced topic that is confusing to programmers who are just learning the basics of a language. For that reason most textbooks provide a collection of classes that hide the exception handling from the programmer. ViewFrame objects are realized as a window. By default, each window has a panel containing an Exit button and a scrolled text area for output. The scrolled text area only has scroll bars when the output cannot all be shown in the window.

We selected the name ViewFrame because a common design pattern for object-oriented programs is the model-view-controller pattern developed by Smalltalk programmers more than 20 years ago. The model is the data of the program, sometimes called its state. The view is what the user sees. The controller is the mechanism used to allow the user to interact with the model. In many programs we combine the view and controller components. A ViewFrame provides that combination for simple programs. In Java, a Frame is a class that is a window. Hence our ViewFrame is a Frame and provides a view component for the program.

The following program is the simplest example of code to create a ViewFrame object called vf. It does nothing with the object except to make it visible—a requirement for all windows. Notice that we must import LabPkg to access its classes.

```
// SimpleVF.java
// Show simple use of a ViewFrame for input and output

import LabPkg.*;

public class SimpleVF
{
  public static void main(String[] args)
  {
    ViewFrame vf = new ViewFrame();
    vf.setVisible(true);

  }
}
```

The code will create the window shown below. The actual window is somewhat larger when initially created.

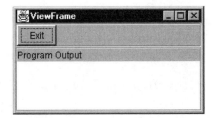

The title of the window is "ViewFrame," which is the default if no title is provided. If a title like "Simple Example" is required, then we create vf with the line

```
ViewFrame vf = new ViewFrame("Simple Example");
```

Input

Input is handled by a number of simple functions that return the desired value. Each takes a string prompt as a parameter. Assuming that we have created a ViewFrame object vf, then examples of input methods are

```
int age = vf.readInt("What is your age?");
double gpa = vf.readDouble("What is your current GPA?");
String name = vf.readString("Enter your name");
```

They all display the prompt in a pop-up dialog box. The user must enter the value in a text field. The first two methods do some error processing for numeric values, forcing the reentry of a value that is of an incorrect format. The first pop-up dialog would be the one shown below:

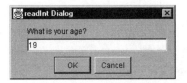

Of course, pop-up dialogs disappear after the information is entered. If you wish to show what was entered on the output, you can include the instruction

```
vf.setIOEcho(true);
```

immediately after creating the ViewFrame object vf. In this case, after the "OK" in the pop-up dialog is clicked, we get the following window display. Notice that the 19 has been echoed to the output window.

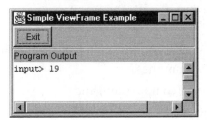

Output

Java provides several methods for output to a console window. Each takes a String parameter.

```
System.out.println("...");
System.out.print("...");
```

The first method inserts a newline (carriage return) after the string parameter value is displayed, while the second one does not.

A ViewFrame object vf has two methods

```
vf.println("...");
```

```
vf.print("...");
```

which function the same way as the console output methods except they display their output in the ViewFrame object's scrolled text area.

The following program reads in two integers and displays their product.

```
// SimpleVF.java
// Show simple use of a ViewFrame for input and output
import LabPkg.*;

public class SimpleVF
{
  public static void main(String[] args)
  {
    ViewFrame vf = new ViewFrame("Simple ViewFrame Example");
    vf.setIOEcho(true);
    vf.setVisible(true);

    int num1 = vf.readInt("What is the first integer?");
    int num2 = vf.readInt("What is the other integer?");
    vf.println("The product is " + (num1 * num2));

  }
}
```

The result of running this program is the window below.

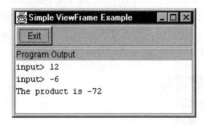

This program does the following:
- creates a ViewFrame object vf, makes it visible, and sets up the echoing of input to the output area
- obtains two values using the readInt methods
- displays a string with the println method
- stops

Although the program stops, the window persists and must be destroyed via the Exit button or the X in the upper-right corner.

For beginners this is a very simple model of a program to follow:
- In main,
  - create a ViewFrame object for input and output,
  - obtain data from the user,
  - perform some computation, and
  - display the results.
- The user will destroy the window after the program terminates and he or she has examined the results.

Buttons   It is often desirable to have a computation repeat as needed. The activation of the computation can be accomplished by clicking on a button provided with a ViewFrame object. In such cases our program takes a different form. It has a class containing a ViewFrame object and the main method for the program just creates an instance of the class. The ViewFrame object is given a button via the method addActionButton.

A template for such a program is provided in the file XXXXXXXX.java, which can be downloaded. It is shown below.

```
// XXXXXXXX.java      replace XXXXXXXX with the class name
//                    and do a "Save As"
// Description:
//
import java.awt.*;
import java.awt.event.*;
import javax.swing.*;
import LabPkg.*;

public class XXXXXXXX
{
    ViewFrame vf;
    public XXXXXXXX()
    {
        vf = new ViewFrame("some title");
        vf.addActionButton(new GeneralButton("button title"));
        //vf.setIOEcho(true);
        vf.setVisible(true);
    }

    ////////////// inner class for a button /////////
    public class GeneralButton extends AbstractAction
    {
        public GeneralButton(String s)
        {
            super(s);
        }

        public void actionPerformed(ActionEvent e)
        {
            // action goes here


        }
    }

    // for simplicity we'll put main right here
    public static void main(String[] args)
    {
        new XXXXXXXX();
    }
}
```

A button requires a listener object. In this template, GeneralButton is a listener. The constructor creates the ViewFrame object vf and then adds the button with the statement

```
vf.addActionButton(new GeneralButton("button title"));
```

A nameless JButton[1] is implicitly created with a GeneralButton object as a listener. This is added to vf. It will appear as a button next to the Exit button with the label given by the string. Of course, you would replace "button title" with the appropriate label.

When the button is clicked, the system calls the special method actionPerformed of the GeneralButton object. This is where the action is! Write the code inside this method for what you wish to happen.

We will convert our example of a program from one that obtains two integers and displays their product to one that does this when a button is pressed. The code is given below. It was created by starting with the template and doing some minor editing (using the Replace option of the editor) to replace all occur-

---

1. A JButton is an extension of the Button class from the AWT package. It is provided with the Swing package.

rences of XXXXXXXX by the name `Product`. Then we added code to the
`actionPerformed` method.

Other changes are indicated in bold.

```java
// Product.java
// Description: Computes a product when a button is pressed
import java.awt.*;
import java.awt.event.*;
import javax.swing.*;
import LabPkg.*;

public class Product
{
    ViewFrame vf;
     public Product()
    {
        vf = new ViewFrame("Product Example");
        vf.addActionButton(new GeneralButton("Compute a Product"));
        vf.setIOEcho(true);
        vf.setVisible(true);
    }

    ////////////// inner class for a button /////////
    public class GeneralButton extends AbstractAction
    {
        public GeneralButton(String s)
        {
            super(s);
        }

        public void actionPerformed(ActionEvent e)
        {
            int num1 = vf.readInt("What is the first integer?");
            int num2 = vf.readInt("What is the other integer?");
            vf.println("The product is " + (num1 * num2));
        }
    }

    // for simplicity we'll put main right here
    public static void main(String[] args)
    {
        new Product();
    }
}
```

When the program is run, a single instance of the class Product is created. It,
in turn, makes its ViewFrame object visible—showing its special button. Now
nothing further will happen unless the button is pressed. As far as main is concerned, its work is over and the Product object persists to do the work. The
visual part of this program is shown below after two presses of the button.

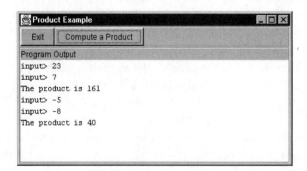

Other buttons could be added. The laboratory "Object-Oriented Java" uses
this model of programming.

Canvas

A ViewFrame object can also contain a Canvas object. This allows the window to display graphical drawings and images. If a Canvas object is created and provided to the constructor for a ViewFrame, then it will be added in the lower part of the frame. **The Canvas object's size must be set or it will default to a 0-by-0 size.**

This is not a critical feature for most programmers, but it does allow us to provide some examples of looping and recursion using drawing on a canvas.

Die

Often we need random whole numbers in a range from 1 to 6 or from 1 to 100. Java provides special classes and methods that provide random numbers from 0.0 to 1.0 and you can do some clever arithmetic to convert these values to whole numbers in the correct range. The Die class takes care of this for you.

Consider code that needs to provide two random integers from 1 to 100, inclusive.

```
Die d = new Die(100);  // specify the upper limit
int n = d.valueOf();// get the initial random value
d.roll();          // change d so it obtains a new random value
int m = d.valueOf();  // get that value
```

The Die class requires that you specify its upper limit at creation. It also obtains its initial random value. The method `valueOf` always returns the current random value maintained in the Die object. The method `roll` is a procedure that causes the Die object to hold a new random value.

The constructor for Die can be given a *seed*. Refer to the online documentation for more information. *Warning:* If two Die objects are created without a seed, it is likely that they will generate the same sequence of values. This happens because Die uses the Random class, which takes the system time as its default seed. The system time used by Java is coarse enough that two Die objects created in the same method are likely to use exactly the same time as their seed.

Useful

The only method in this class is `pause`, which takes a single integer parameter representing (in tenths of a second) how long to pause execution. Typical use is

```
Useful.pause(25);   // wait 2.5 second before going on
```

This is valuable when you want a component to appear on the screen prior to doing some drawing on it.

Other Classes

The class `CanvasWithMsg` extends `Canvas` and displays a string centered on the canvas.

The `QuitAction` provides the Exit button in a ViewFrame, while `HandleWindowDeath` is a listener class for closing of the ViewFrame window. Most beginning programmers will never explicitly use them.

APPENDIX B

IDE Information

Kawa

Kawa is available for download from the URL

`http://www.allaire.com/products/kawa/index.cfm`

It requires installation of Sun Microsystems' free SDK 2. (Version 1.2 or higher is needed for use with LabPkg.) It does not require project creation for single file programs.

Kawa IDE Commands

Task	Menu Selection or Action	Shortcut
Open a file	File>Open	Ctrl + O
Create a file	File>New	Ctrl + N
Save As	File>Save As	
Compile a file	Build>Compile	F7
Compile a project	Build>Rebuild All	Shift + F7
Create a project	Project>New	
Open a project	Project>Open	
Close a project	Right-click on the project name and select "close"	
Run a program	Build>Run	F4
Print a file	File>Print	Ctrl + P

For proper execution of the program, the project file and the files in the project should be in the same folder.

JBuilder

JBuilder is available from Borland in various forms. The basic version is JBuilder Foundation. Refer to the URL

`http://www.borland.com/jbuilder/`

for download information.

JBuilder does not provide very many keyboard shortcuts other than the standard Windows menu navigation mechanism, which is typically invoked by typing the [Alt] key followed by the first letter of the menu and then some letter (indicated by an underline in the menu item names) in the command you wish to select.

JBuilder IDE Commands

Task	Menu Selection or Action
Open a file	File>Open
Create a file	File>New
Save As	File>Save As
Compile a file	Project>Make <file name>
Compile a project	Project>Make <project name>
Create a project	File>New Project
Open a project	File>Open Project
Close a project	File>Close Projects
Run a program	Run>Run Project
Print a file	File>Print <file name>

VisualCafé

VisualCafé is available from WebGain, Inc., at the URL

`http://www.webgain.com/Products/VisualCafe_Overview.html`

VisualCafé IDE Commands

Task	Menu Selection or Action	Shortcut
Open a file	File>Open	[Ctrl] + O
Create a file	File>New File	[Ctrl] + N
Save As	File>Save As	
Compile a file	Project>Compile {file name}	[Ctrl] + [F7]
Compile a project	Project>Rebuild All or Project>Build Application	[F7]
Create a project	File>New Project	[Ctrl] + [Shift] + N
Open a project	File>Open Project	[Ctrl] + [Shift] + O

VisualCafé IDE Commands

Task	Menu Selection or Action	Shortcut
Close a project	File>Close Project	
Run a program	Project>Execute	Ctrl + F5
Print a file	File>Print	Ctrl + P

When a project is created, the options must be set via Project>Options. The main class should be specified along with the executable. Normally, if the class containing main is D, then the main class is D and the executable is D.exe.

Read the documentation on how to access a package like LabPkg for a project.

CodeWarrior

The CodeWarrior IDE supports development in Java, C++, and Pascal. Because of this it is slightly more difficult to use, but meets the needs of students who program in both Java and C++. Information is available from Metrowerks at the URL

http://www.metrowerks.com/desktop/java/

CodeWarrior IDE Commands

Task	Menu Selection or Action	Shortcut
Open a file	File>Open, select files of type "Source Files"	Ctrl + O
Create a file	File>New	Ctrl + N
Save As	File>Save As	
Compile a file	Project>Compile	Ctrl + F7
Compile a project	Project>Make	F7
Create a project	see note below	Ctrl + Shift + N
Open a project	File>Open, select files of type "Project Files"	Ctrl + O
Close a project	Kill the project window	
Run a program	Project>Run	
Print a file	File>Print	Ctrl + P

Creating a project is best accomplished in CodeWarrior by using one of the Java template projects provided by CodeWarrior. Start with the template "Java Application." Give the project a name. All CodeWarrior projects automatically create a folder using the project name, so be sure you place the project folder where you want it on your hard drive.

Once created, the project window shows two groups of files: Source and Classes. There is a single file, TrivialApplication.java, under the Source category. We suggest that you simply delete it from the project by right-clicking on it. Then create the appropriate files and add them to the project with Source highlighted. Files of the project need not be in the project folder. You should add the file LabPkg.jar to the Classes category. The file may be copied from the `Setup` folder of the diskette that accompanies this book.

You will want to change the various settings of the project to match the file names.

Index